Milk, Meltdowns, and a Mediocre Mummy

Memoirs of a mini-human

Louise King

HEDDON PUBLISHING

www.heddonpublishing.com

www.facebook.com/heddonpublishing

@PublishHeddon

For Emily

I'm hoping one day you will read this and it will make you smile (and maybe apologise...)

I love you completely.

Mummy xxx

Louise King is actually a pen name (a pretty uninspiring one at that), because Louise is actually a head of science at a high school and doesn't want her pupils or their parents to know she wrote this, as it includes quite a lot of swearing and mentions of her breasts.

She is a fairly normal, over-thinking, over-sharing 35-year-old woman living somewhere in the north-west of the UK. She doesn't have any pets, because she can only just about keep children alive and has killed every plant she has ever tried to grow.

When not on parental duty, she enjoys drinking (alcohol and hot tea), dancing to 90s and 00s pop, eating chocolate, and actually completing conversations with her glorious friends.

She still can't quite believe she has written a book (which is of course entirely, completely, absolutely, without-any-doubt, a work of fiction, and not based on any actual events).

The first month:

Survival

12th January

What the actual feck!

I am currently getting a sodding nipple shoved up my nose, when I am pretty sure it should be in my mouth, after *the* most horrific experience known to man. I have been squashed and squeezed and manhandled out into a freezing cold abyss. After being forcefully expelled, I was greeted with, 'Shitting hell! Oh shit! That's the first words it'll hear.'

Incorrect.

The first words I heard were the forced and idle chit-chat that was taking place as my head was dangling out of the cosiness of the birth canal (pretty sure I've ensured it won't be quite that cosy ever again) for an agonisingly long five minutes between contractions as my mother's foot was perched, I must admit rather daintily, on the midwife's shoulder. Hardly the rapturous welcome I had imagined.

To top it all off, I'm now covered in blood, with a

ridiculous itchy thing on my head, whilst my rather haggard-looking mummy is just staring at me like I'm some sort of alien life-form. I think she's one to avoid at all costs.

The man whom I assume is the "daddy" they keep referring to hasn't fared much better. When asked what I am, he fails to even determine my gender for a good ten seconds. Potentially another one to steer clear of.

Then they cut my cord without asking. Rude.

Then I got weighed. Exceptionally cold.

Then I got jabbed with a needle.

Not a great start.

13th January

Well, it didn't get much better last night. I've learnt that both Mummy and Daddy are in fact, rather disappointingly, mine for keeps. They're both bloody clueless, so I'm holding out for one of those hospital mix-ups at some point soon.

Mummy didn't even know she had to dress me, and had to be condescendingly prompted by the healthcare assistant to do so. She also had to be prompted to change my nappy when I'd unleashed my first faecal deposit. And my clothes, when I was sick on myself. I'll be honest, I've got very little faith in her. She looks completely fecking shell-shocked, if truth to be told. Although, she was pretty good at religiously setting an alarm to feed me every three hours. Not that she needed the alarm. She just spent the night staring at me and touching my chest every ten minutes, to check I was breathing.

Daddy also still seems a bit lacking. He's holding me like he's scared he's going to break me, which isn't filling me with confidence. But at least he looks at me as though he actually likes me, unlike Mummy. I think she's off her tits on drugs, and seems more worried about her own first faecal deposit than anything else.

The day got better when the rest of my family arrived. Grandma, Grandad and Nanny have obviously done this before, as their cuddles were delightful, so that gave me

3

some hope. My uncles clearly don't have a fecking clue and held me like I was a plank of wood. My auntie was somewhat of a middle ground.

Mummy is still shoving her nipple up my nose whilst an array of women tell her to wait for me to open really wide and to establish "a good latch". I'm opening as wide as I bloody can. I don't think they quite understand that I just want milk, I don't really give a shite what my latch is like. Then she keeps taking photos of her nipples after I've fed, to show these ladies that they are in fact quite lipstick-shaped so *I* must be doing something wrong. I'm less than a day old. How can it possibly be my fault?

14th January

I "came home" today. It smells quite strange, but at least I'm free from that vivarium of a post-natal ward. I couldn't handle how sweaty it was making Mummy and Daddy. They didn't help themselves by trying to wrestle me into an ill-advised "going home outfit", right before I vommed up my feed and subsequently pooed. I mean, who thinks dungarees on a new-born are a good idea?!

Then they strapped me into the car seat. Sweet baby Jesus! They nearly broke my ribs, I could barely breathe, and there was definitely not two fingers' room underneath those straps! Mummy's idea of car safety and the midwife's were thankfully different and I was rescued with a tactful 'Shall we just loosen them a little?'

The car journey home was actually quite nice. I had a lovely little snooze. Mummy stared anxiously at me, tensing and gripping her crotch, whilst Daddy only semi-successfully dodged the potholes.

After we got home, my great-uncle, great-auntie and great-cousins came round to visit. Despite their grand titles, I liked them. It was all about cuddles, some awesome presents, and being told that I was beautiful.

Then it all went a bit downhill. Mummy lost the plot and Daddy found her crying in the kitchen because she'd bled all over the bathmat after having a bath to soothe her stitches and piles. All this whilst leaking milk profusely from her suddenly gargantuan breasts. Apparently, all of this is my fault. The fecking audacity! I'm the one that has to struggle to latch on to the bloody engorged things! It's like a weird game of apple-bobbing, made considerably more difficult by the vats of slippery lanolin she's perpetually slathering on.

Then Mummy said she doesn't love me yet. And then she cried about that as well. She needs to give herself a break. I don't love her yet. Not even close. It's only been two days, for feck's sake, and she's hardly given a strong account of herself so far.

15th January

Cord-gate. Mummy knocked it a tad during my top-and-tail today, and all fecking hell broke loose. I was crying, she was crying, Daddy was trying to calm everyone down. It was carnage. If I'm honest, I probably over-exaggerated my response a little, but I was cold, naked and hungry, so I think that can be forgiven.

Mummy got Daddy to ring her friend Niccy (because she's a wonderful midwife), as she couldn't possibly voice what she'd done out loud, because she was so upset, and then Daddy had to take a photo to send to Niccy, but not on Mummy's phone, as she couldn't bear to see the damaged, semi-rotten umbilicus photo ever again.

It was all fine in the end, and it's still currently clinging on. The bloody thing falls off anyway at some point, so not quite sure what all the drama was about! Although I now share Mummy's concern that I'll end up with an "outy".

16th January

Mummy and Daddy have finally succumbed and bought something called a 'Sleepyhed'. They used the money that *I'd* been given for the ordeal of being born, without even asking me. Trying to justify it with, 'Well, she will use it,' to ease their consciences. Bloody thieves.

Mind you, they both look absolutely knackered. They keep saying they are, at least. I can't actually see them properly yet as my vision hasn't developed enough. I'm not surprised they're knackered, as they're being completely bloody ridiculous at night-time. I'm obviously refusing to go in my Snoozepod - why would I want to go in there? It's massive and empty, and smells funny. They try and trick me by letting me drift off to sleep on them, all warm and cosy, and then attempt to sneak me into the Snoozepod. No chance – I'm wise to their devious ways! I wake and scream immediately, at just the right pitch and volume to ensure my swift removal to the safety of their exhausted arms.

This way, I get to sleep all cuddled up on either my mummy or daddy, whilst they force themselves to stay awake in two-hourly slots, just watching me, or scrolling through the NHS and sleep-safe websites, as they're terrified I'll immediately die if they drift off, or if the room temperature increases by more than 0.1°c on the Gro-egg. Consequently, I have upgraded my previous judgement of my parents from Bloody Clueless to Absolute Fecking Morons.

Anyway, back to the Sleepyhed. Apparently, this is going to solve all of their problems, as it will magically mimic being snuggled with them. They must think I'm bloody stupid. What a waste of my money!

Whilst they were excitedly anticipating an increased amount of slumber this evening, they got a bit giddy and decided to give me a bath. I can't stand the old top-and-tail at the best of times, so I don't know why they thought a full immersion into water would go down well.

Mummy was obviously very anxious about it all so rang Niccy again (poor sod) and wrote down step-by-step instructions on the back of an envelope. She even wrote down "run water". I should have known then it would not end well.

To summarise, there was a lot of screaming, tears and anxiety from all involved, culminating in, 'We'll stick to the top-and-tail for a while.' Correct choice, parents. At least my cord is still beautifully rotting and intact... just!

It got to bedtime, and we all retired to the bedroom. Mummy tried the old trick of feeding and cuddling me till I was all dopey and sleepy, and I could almost taste the adrenaline as they prepared for the transition to this Sleepyhed contraption. *Right*, I thought, *here we go*. I geared myself up for a proper scream but, holy shite, this thing was amazing! It cushioned me in all the right places and didn't wriggle and move when it got a dead arm. No coughing. No staring at me. Perfection!

17th January

After a myriad of visitors in the last couple of days, I was beginning to think Mummy and Daddy were getting the general gist of this parenting lark. We'd even ventured out in my outrageously priced pram for a short walk, as Mummy shuffled along trying to surreptitiously support her sagging perineum without making the neighbours think she was touching herself. And then, *bang!* I got clunked on the head by the fridge door as my mummy forgot it swung backwards.

She cried so much anyone would think it was her who'd been hit on the head. Well, actually, she did end up getting hit on the head with the fridge door, because she went into a state of panic and thought that I was immediately going to die. First, she made Daddy put his head there and swung the door so he could say how hard it had hit me. Not believing him when he said it wasn't that bad, she then made him swing the fridge door into her head. I just watched on, with my limited visual acuity. What a pair of plonkers.

Mummy was so upset, she couldn't even ring Grandma to decide whether to rush me to hospital, so was WhatsApping her instead. Her hands were that sweaty from the whole ordeal, she dropped the phone on my face.

That is when I really lost my shite.

Grandma's recommendation was a glass of wine – for Mummy, not me. Mummy was worried how this would look when Social Services inevitably and immediately came to take me away, due to the fridge door incident. Something tells she me is slightly anxious. Probably the hormones.

The day did not get any better as the midwife came, sliced half my foot off, and squeezed blood out. She also said I have gained weight, which apparently is a good thing. Mummy seemed unjustifiably proud of herself.

20th January

Had a ridiculous "second Christmas" today because another great-cousin was here to see me, and she missed actual Christmas. As far as I can tell, Christmas is where a lot of people get together in a strange house and make a shedload of noise; crinkling paper, clanking cutlery, popping corks, and shouting over each other. I knew early doors it wasn't really for me, so decided to scream. And scream. And scream.

Finally, Daddy got the message, and thought I'd be better off upstairs out of the way, where I could settle and gorge myself on milk. Daddy seems a nervous one and doesn't like me in strange places where I might be uncomfortable, bless him. Mummy appeared a bit gutted to be missing out on all the noise. It's not like she's been pretty much housebound for eight days.

The best bit of the day was going to meet my great-grandparents. They are awesome. My great-grandma was lovely, albeit very bony, which was quite uncomfortable during the cuddle, but I decided to let it slide because at least she was quiet.

My great-grandad is hilarious! He asked numerous times whether I'd been found under a gooseberry bush, told my Daddy what a huge mistake he'd made, and kept calling me Emma. I mean, I quite like the name Emma. It's a timeless classic. And as he correctly pointed out, it's only a 'mily' difference.

24th January

Met James today. My "boyfriend", apparently. As far as I could see, which is still not much at all, he looked alright, and seemed really good at sleeping all day, so at least we have something in common. We met him at the pub with his parents, who were in the same NCT (bloody middle-class parents) group as us. They've gone rogue and met up outside of the established group. If this is the height of their rebelliousness, I think I can cope.

Mummy seemed very nervous about it all and didn't want to appear too keen or desperate, and thus found herself in quite the present-giving quandary:

A) They buy a present for me, and we haven't bought one for James – we would appear mean and stingy. The worst outcome.

B) We buy a present for James, and they haven't bought one for me because they'd forgotten – we would make them feel terrible. Not great.

C) We buy a present for James, and they haven't bought one for me because they didn't think it necessary. We would appear too eager and needy, as we barely know them, thus we would be exiled from their friendship forever more.

In the end, she went with buying a present, hiding it in the bottom of the pram, and presenting it when they gave theirs. It was actually quite genius.

This does not begin to equal how nervous she appears to be about feeding in public, though. I have decided to be kind, and haven't inflicted it on her just yet (the one in the layby near the Audi garage doesn't count, as we were in the car, although a white van man did cop a good eyeful). I let her enjoy her glass of Sauvignon (is it bad that I already know my grape varieties?) and tell her "birth story".

As first dates go, it went quite well, although it did end with some chat about how James and I were going to get married. They took photos of us together, because they'd be so cute to show on the wedding day. I'm not sure I'm on board for the whole arranged marriage. I'm just not ready to commit yet.

25th January

I couldn't put it off any longer. I demanded to be fed in public today. I chose my venue wisely... Tesco's café.

Mummy is still leaking everywhere, so it is quite the palaver, and she doesn't half feck about. First, she had to Infacol me. Then she has to unclip an array of tops and bras to subsequently tuck a muslin into said bra, remove her soaked breast pad (and place it somewhere she will inevitably forget or knock it down from), slather on the lanolin, and finally try and get me to latch on. All whilst Daddy looked on helplessly, rooting around in the bag for god knows what.

Needless to say, it was not a smooth operation. I got sprayed in the eye a number of times, and Mummy exposed herself to a group of disabled adults and their carers. At least 50% of them were partially sighted, so they probably didn't see too much, which I suppose is of some consolation.

26th January

Today, Mummy took me out in the car by herself - a first. She wasn't quite prepared for the bright January sunshine that was beaming directly into my eyes so, as well as pulling over regularly to check I was still breathing, she was also yelling, 'Close your eyes, protect your retinas!' every time we turned a corner. Not the most peaceful of journeys.

We went to Niccy's house, and I got to meet her daughter Edie. I'll be honest, she wasn't that interested in me. To be fair, she is only one year old, and I do very little, so I won't hold it against her for now.

Niccy, being the oracle of all things baby, had been roped in to helping with the very important task of making a card with my footprint on for Daddy's birthday. I'm really glad she was there as Mummy, true to form, was clueless, and very uncreative. In the end, we've made a card that says, "You're the best Daddy by par". This "hilarious" pun was Mummy's only real contribution, and she obviously feels very proud, although I'm not sure she can claim any credit as she found it on Pinterest. I mean, it's fine, but I'm not sure Mummy realises that Daddy is more bothered about getting actual pars than a card with my footprint depicting the fairway.

27th January

I NEED MILK!

I can't quite explain it, but this incessant urge to feed has possessed me. Maybe it's one of those "growth spurts" the midwives keep talking about. It's fine, though, because my mummy still has an ample supply, so I can gorge all the live-long day. I've got a slight competitive streak in me, so I beat my own record this evening and fed thirteen times in five hours.

I'm getting the slight impression my mummy doesn't like feeding me, though. Each time I'm hungry and I go through all the textbook moves: sticking my tongue out; turning my head to whoever's chest I'm on; generally rooting around, and finally crying, Daddy will say, 'I think she needs a feed,' and Mummy will slightly hysterically say, 'No, nope, no, no she doesn't. I think it's nappy/wind/colic/tiredness [delete as applicable].'

My daddy then tries treating all of these, which just angers me even more, before Mummy concedes that I actually do need feeding. Then she slathers more lanolin on her already exposed boobs (she's learnt not to bother putting them away) and I attempt to latch on, whilst she winces with what I can only assume is utter joy at this wonderful bonding process.

29th January

Over the last few days, I have developed a bit of a gunky eye. Some do-gooder told Mummy the best way to sort it was to put breastmilk in it. Unfortunately, they didn't tell her precisely how to achieve this, and left it up to her to figure it out. Mistake. Rather than use a cotton pad like any normal mother would do, mine decided the only possible way was to dangle her still-enormous breast over my eye and try and squeeze and aim at the same time, whilst Daddy held me still. She managed to knock Daddy's glasses so hard it made his nose bleed.

Thus, I ended up being held by a bleeding father whilst a swinging, squirting breast was soaking me in milk with a 10% accuracy ratio.

Give me strength.

Needless to say, the eye is still gunky.

30th January

Mummy has a cold, so wasn't able to meet up with all her new NCT friends that she paid for. She actually cried because she is worried that they will all instantly bond at this first post-baby meeting, and then won't possibly be able to accept her into the clique, and she will be NCT-friendless forever more, and won't survive maternity leave. For feck's sake.

1st February

Been feeling a bit grotty today, as I'm all bunged up, and have no way of clearing it. I can't blow my own nose; I can't take any medicines; I can't hock it up. I've realised I'm very ill-equipped to deal with this.

All Mummy and Daddy do is continuously squirt bloody saline spray up my nose. And they have a similar accuracy ratio at this as they did with the breast milk in the eye, so no wonder I'm not getting better!

On the plus side, I got registered as official today! Hurrah! You'd think this would be a joyous occasion for all, but apparently not. As soon as we left, Mummy started to panic about my middle name. At one point, I think she was close to tears. Daddy didn't know what to do, in that he let Mummy pick it in the first place. It was completely ridiculous. No one uses the fecking thing anyway. And the worst case is some mild playground mocking if it's really, really shite.

It was Daddy's birthday, so after him being thoroughly underwhelmed by the footprint-card (much to Mummy's disappointment), we celebrated the day with a cheeky Nando's. Daddy had a photo of him posing with a beer in one hand and me in the other, looking like he's loving life. What a cliché. And a lie. This picture does not tell the tale of how wound up he gets when I leak shit onto my clothes all the time.

2nd February

Three weeks old today, so I decided to celebrate with an A&E trip and an ambulance ride. I'd been missing the security that being around health professionals gives. It was also Daddy's first day back at work and I didn't want him to go.

He managed to spend an hour and a half in uniform before he got a call to say an ambulance was on its way because I was struggling to breathe. Struggling is a bit of an exaggeration; I would say it was more intermittent breathlessness. After 111 decided an ambulance was necessary, I got a bit tired with all the heavy breathing, and went for a sleep. I made sure I looked extra cute and a picture of health for when the paramedics arrived, as first impressions count.

Despite my angelic sleeping face, they took one look at the video my mummy took of my breathing and said I needed to go to A&E, so I got an awesome trip in an ambulance. Which I obviously slept through.

3rd February

Managed to get a free night's stay in hospital. Daddy was not so lucky. He had to stay in his own bed, unlike Mummy, who got a delightful hospital one whilst monitoring my heart rate all night and freaking out when an alarm told her my oxygen saturation levels were dropping every fifteen minutes.

The lovely doctor said I have bronchiolitis and I just need monitoring at home. So back we came, and I'm being watched like a hawk by everyone.

Fortunately, the doctor told Mummy that she should use a cotton pad for the breastmilk in my eye, rather than the swing-and-squirt technique, so at least I'm not being put through that ordeal anymore.

6th February

Heard Mummy telling Grandma that she felt like she had nailed motherhood this morning.

Apparently, feeding is getting easier, she'd managed to have a shower, and sterilise some bottles, *and* she had even cleaned the dishwasher filters (for the first time ever).

Pride comes before a fall, my friend!

While she was trying to get us out of the house to meet her NCT friends, I produced a poo, prompting a nappy change, then another poo – hence another nappy change – and then demanded in no uncertain terms that I be fed. She was late, and put rightfully back in her place.

This didn't prevent her telling everyone her "birth story" again. It doesn't get any more interesting. Nobody is that bothered that the train barriers came down on the way to the hospital. Or that the local school had just kicked out and the children were crossing the road like a stream of endless lemmings that Daddy had considered mowing down.

Yes, you wanted an epidural and couldn't get one.

Yes, you needed stitches, and sounded like Barry White on the gas and air.

Who cares?

There was then the full round of birth stories, with the

exception of one mummy, who was still waiting for her baby to come, and had been for thirteen days. She had started off complaining how she just wanted to go into labour now. This line seemed to dry up once she'd heard birth story number four.

Obviously, everyone's was horrific and painful, and blah, blah, blah. With the exception of Phillipa. Her waterbirth was an NCT leader's wet dream. Whilst all the mummies said how glad they were about her perfect birth, something in their tone suggested they would quite like Phillipa to shut the feck up. Especially when she said her baby Finley had latched on with seconds, fed like a dream, and was sleeping through the night. Your eyebags say different, Phillipa, my friend.

The catch-up ended with one brave, albeit guilty-looking, mummy saying, 'What's the worst thing you've called your baby so far? Mine is twat!'

There was a chorus of relieved sighs from around the table. After which a whole torrent of foul language erupted. Worryingly, a lot came from Mummy. And obviously none from Phillipa, who nearly choked on her decaf, soya, tasteless crappy latte.

8th February

Mummy and Daddy left me today! I'll concede that it was for a good reason, as Daddy had a hospital appointment. And it was only for an hour. And it was with Grandma, who is much more experienced than them anyway. But still.

I've decided I really like Grandma. Not only does she tell me I'm beautiful every time I see her, but she is funny. She is convinced she is the one that can get me to take a dummy. Absolutely no bloody chance! Why would I want a fake silicone nipple in my mouth? Sometimes I play with her a bit and suck it for thirty seconds or so. Then I gag and retch and spit it out. She's determined, though. And resilient. I'll give her that.

Anyway, Mummy had expressed some milk (she was panicked she might affect her supply by expressing two ounces. Ha! She clearly doesn't know what I have in store), but fed me just before they left and said I definitely wouldn't need it. Well, that planted the seed of hunger, so within fifteen minutes, I was screaming, demanding to be fed. Grandma managed to get the bottle into me pretty quickly, and it was delicious. Best milk I've ever tasted. Despite the silicone nipple.

9th February

After sleeping for five hours straight in the night, in spite of Mummy's alarm going off to wake me to feed (she decided not to, after copious amounts of Googling), I felt on top of the world today.

We went to Grandma's house for an "I'm showing off my amazingly gorgeous new granddaughter to all my friends" party. Grandma, ever the organiser, had given her friends time slots where they could come have a cuppa, cake, and a cuddle with me.

In order to increase my gorgeous factor, Mummy manhandled me into a pair of dungarees (evidently, she hasn't learned her lesson from the last time), and put socks on me. What a ridiculous piece of clothing they are.

Anyway, to summarise the party in Daddy's words, I basically "got passed around like a joint". Grandma's friends arrived (obviously at their allotted times) and then lined up to hold me, whilst exclaiming how cute/beautiful/gorgeous/wonderful I was, and how well my mummy looked.

I thought I was going to have to hear The Birth Story umpteen times but luckily was spared, as Mummy didn't seem overly keen to talk about her torn vagina so openly with this crowd.

The whole party passed very quickly, in a haze of decorative scarves, long necklaces, and floral perfume. I think I slept on and off for the whole day, which is good, as it means I can stay up longer in the middle of night tonight.

Month 2:

All about the milk

15th February

I've been ridiculously hungry in the last couple of days, and have managed to increase Mummy's milk supply massively. I'll admit, I may have got carried away and gone a little too far, as it's just never-ending. So much so, Mummy's nipples taste of cabbage from the leaves she's weirdly been shoving on her breasts.

In hindsight, I maybe didn't need to feed every hour for three nights in a row. I'm now struggling to get any suction on her nipples, despite being held in a variety of different positions. Including the "rugby ball", which I find a little offensive. Not to worry, though, there's so much that it just pours out and I can lap at it with my tongue. Perfect.

Apparently, the feeding consultant that came out to see us says this isn't good, and thinks I have a tongue-tie. Never heard of it. But I did hear the phrases "small snip", "almost painless", and "not much blood". I am going to assume that this in relation to Daddy, seeing as he says 'We're never having another one!' so often.

My eye is still mega-gunky and sometimes when I wake up, I can't open it properly. I couldn't give less of a shit, as I can't see much anyway, and when I can it's mostly Mummy's worried face gazing forlornly at my eye. But this is clearly upsetting Mummy, and she has taken to squidging the gunk out of my eye and wiping it incessantly. Daddy has had to limit her to two wipes a day. She sneaks at least another four in whilst he's at work.

16th February

What a lovely day I've had. After the usual early morning permitted eye-wipe (and a few cheeky extras when Daddy was upstairs), we went for a lovely, snuggly drive and visited a shopping centre and a pub.

Because I've been feeding so much, Mummy is producing a ridiculous amount of milk and was in agony as we walked around the shops. Being as unprepared as ever, she had to ask a young, naïve barista in Costa to lend her a paper cup, and then had to hand-express in the toilets of a pub. I fear she is not the classiest of ladies.

I'm not sure where this milk went. I think I heard her tell Daddy she poured it down the sink. But surely nobody would be so stupid as to dispose of such liquid gold that way?

18th February

Not much to report. Eyes still gunky. Feeding takes me much longer now, which is great as I get extra cuddles.

Hilariously, Daddy told Mummy that seven hours of unbroken daytime sleep after a night shift was way worse than four hours' broken sleep during the night. I drifted off as I gazed happily into Mummy's bulging, rolling eyes.

20th February

Finding it harder and harder to latch onto Mummy's ever-growing breasts, it's taking thirty-five minutes a feed, which is not ideal, as I have lots of other important things to be doing: sleeping; shuffling around in my bed; improving my vision; practising my smiles; vomiting.

At least I can still poo whilst I feed. Now that's multi-tasking.

The good thing is, it does mean I'm feeding pretty much non-stop, so at least Mummy can join me in my lack of sleep. And Daddy is working nights, so it's just the two of us, and we get lots of bonding time. She says my name, and some other choice words, the most if I drift off a little bit after a feed then wake just after. I find eleven minutes is the optimum time interval for this. It gives her just enough time to go to the toilet, quickly check WhatsApp, and Google "is it normal for my baby to feed non-stop?" and then, just as she thinks this might be the chance to sleep herself, I shuffle, stir, cry, and need to feed again.

23rd February

Another Friday, another free night's stay in hospital! And this time I got Daddy in as well. And they got free tuna sandwiches, so you think they'd be more grateful.

My breathing went funny again, and then I did the most epic vom to date (it was seriously impressive), so they packed me off to A&E. This time, I actually did let the doctors see my laboured breathing, so I got taken straight to this lovely ward. It was cosy, and I got to stay in a plastic box again, which brought back bitter-sweet memories of birth.

I wasn't so pleased with the blood sample and chest X-ray, but by far the worst bit was when they tried to shove a tube up my nose. The first time, they didn't even lubricate it. Anyway, in the end, with lubrication, they still couldn't pass the tube up my nose, and it came out covered in blood, so apparently my nasal passage might not have formed fully or something. I blame the odd glass of wine, and occasional prawns, that Mummy had whilst pregnant. I'm sure she went to a 'Moules-a-go-go' once as well.

At least I made the doctor feel bad by smiling non-stop at him just before he assaulted my nasal passage.

24th February

Got home today and Mummy and Daddy both burst into tears. What the feck? I'm the one with the violated, dodgy nose. Apparently, it was the relief of being home, and me being alive. Jesus, they don't half make a meal of things. Granted, they only had an hour's sleep, sharing a single hospital bed, but still. They need to pull themselves together.

Grandma and Grandad came round to keep their retired-GP-eyes on me whilst Mummy and Daddy went for some sleep. Had the usual dummy battle with Grandma, which obviously I won. I think Grandad is beginning to find me slightly more interesting, but I can tell he wants me to do a bit more. I mean, I smile at him, and track the toy he waves in front of my face. What more does he bloody want?

26th February

Had to go back to my favourite place: the hospital. Although this time it was a scheduled visit, as apparently I might have dodgy hips to match my dodgy nasal passage. I was exceptionally brave in the face of some jelly being rubbed on my hips, and an ultrasound being completed, or so the kind lady said. The scariest bit was when the sonographer's "helper" tried to force my nappy back on – she made Mummy look positively competent, as she didn't have a fecking clue, and left a bum cheek exposed. Needless to say, I took full advantage, with a well-timed poo in the car, which escaped the confines of my vest and baby-gro, and seeped into the car seat.

27th February

Oh my god, I have boobs! Well, I should say "a boob", as it's just the left one. I knew I was quite mature for my age, but I didn't think this would happen yet. Amazing! I'll be the envy of all the other babies, providing they even themselves out.

Otherwise, I'll just end up lop-sided, like Mummy.

Obviously, this development induced a panic in my mummy, thinking I'd developed breast cancer. When have you ever heard of a baby having breast cancer? Jesus. She's decided it's just something to do with her oestrogen that has got into my body, causing my breast tissue to temporarily enlarge. I am ignoring her. They're here to stay, I'm sure of it.

28th February

Mummy took me to my first baby class today. She was beside herself with nervous excitement, which was very embarrassing; obviously, she doesn't understand the concept of playing it cool. We went with two of Mummy's NCT friends and their babies, Sophie and Jasper. Jasper is the trendiest baby I know. Sophie and I went a bit shy when we saw him rocking his dinosaur pants and matching bib.

Anyway, back to the class. It's called Rhythm Time, and is run by just the most fantastic lady I have ever met. Andrea. She has beautiful greying hair, and I couldn't take my eyes off her the whole time. This seemed to irk Mummy somewhat, as I was meant to be bonding with her. But she has the most terrible voice, while Andrea has the voice of an angel. And I might never see Andrea again, or get to listen to her delightful melodies again, so I had to make the most of it. I loved every second.

2nd March

Argh! An annoying day all round. Firstly, the boobs have gone. Turns out Mummy was right about the hormones, as she keeps proudly telling anyone who will listen.

Secondly, I really fecking hate the dangling objects on my playmat that Mummy is constantly lying me on in a bid to "stimulate" me.

It's not as though it's easy for me to hit them. I have virtually no control over any of my limbs, and it's pure dumb luck if I do manage to hit one. Then, every time I do, it just swings right back. And keeps swinging. Making it even harder for me to hit it again! ARGH!

Even worse, Mummy seems to be in awe of me intermittently hitting these ridiculous hanging things and says she's watching me learn, "it's just amazing". I mean, talk about low standards. If she's impressed by this, I do worry about her aspirations for me, long-term.

On a positive note, there's no denying she definitely loves me now. Particularly when I smile at her. She goes crazy for it.

5th March

Met up with some of the NCT babies today, and turns out I am being way too nice to my parents. James in particular gave me some great tips on screaming and crying all day at home, to really drive them mad. It seems the crux of it is to be an angel in public, so that people don't believe your parents. I love the fact he's such a rebel.

With James' wisdom fresh in my mind, I thought I'd try it out. I screamed. And screamed. And screamed. Pretty much all afternoon. It didn't matter what Mummy did, I just went for it. It was quite amusing to see all the different tactics she would use to try and calm me.

She even whacked out this swinging blanket she got conned into buying at a baby event before I arrived. I let her think she'd got her money's worth for maybe seven minutes... then started up again.

As fun as it is to watch Mummy scrabble about for new ideas to quieten me, it is rather tiring, so I fell asleep in the end. Unfortunately, it was at the time when Mummy was trying the tactic of whispering my name over and over again, which was in fact just very annoying and boring, but she now thinks that this was some sort of parenting triumph, so no doubt I'll have to endure this for the next couple of days.

7th March

So it turns out that it wasn't Daddy and a potential vasectomy that they were talking about a couple of weeks ago... it's me who's had the snip. And I am not impressed.

I genuinely cannot believe my parents allowed this to happen to me. I mean, yes, I didn't really feel anything. And yes, there was barely any blood. And yes, already I can feed better. And, OK, yes, I've had great fun playing with my awesome newly-untethered tongue. But still! They let a stranger (albeit a highly trained stranger) cut my frenulum (that I was rather attached to) with blunt-ended scissors. Blunt-ended! Not even sharp.

Worse still... Mummy was that upset that when they handed me back to her, she couldn't even comfort me properly, despite the frenulum-snipper telling her to. She kept dripping tears onto me as I fed. She cried more than me. This seems to be a developing theme. The plus side was that she forgot to keep whispering my name repeatedly (which she has been doing ever since its supposed success a few day ago) so every cloud.

I dealt with 'the snip' or frenotomy like such a legend that Mummy felt up to taking me to my Rhythm Time class and Grandma came, too. Andrea, my hero, was there again, and I just basked in her presence and got swept away with her beautiful voice. My favourite song is Pop it in the Basket, as it's both upbeat and helpfully instructional. Even Mummy can't get that one wrong.

9th March

My doubts regarding my parents' capabilities have heightened further. Today, they've let "Nurse Debra" jab me three times in the leg. It fricking hurt, as well. The needles were mahoosive; I genuinely thought they might come out of the other side of my leg.

I cried. Mummy cried (shocker). Daddy didn't like it much, either.

Then they debated for about twenty minutes about when it was best to give me Calpol... errrr, how about straight away?!

Once I'd had the sweet pink nectar, I felt a bit better, and threw a few smiles about, as I was feeling generous and I actually really like doing it. I felt that OK, I even enjoyed a bit of "swing and mostly miss" on the playmat for ten minutes. I was not that OK that I enjoyed bloody "tummy time", though.

Daddy went off to work nights, so Mummy's friend Penny came round to help out, cook tea, and drink wine. Apparently, her daughter was terrible, so she knew how to handle a screaming baby, should I get worse. I thought I'd take her down a peg or two. Turns out, she was EPIC at handling a screaming baby, and had me asleep within fifteen minutes, every time she held me. Her daughter is one lucky lady!

I was that exhausted from some intense scream sessions

(when Mummy thought she could handle it before deferring to Penny) that I slept for nine hours. I feel I've let myself down, allowing Mummy to sleep. Although she did keep setting an alarm to check on me, so at least she didn't get that much.

11th March

Apparently today was a big deal: "Mother's Day"? And Mummy felt very let down. I think she probably had set her expectations too high (for a change). From what I heard her tell Grandma, Daddy made a number of errors:

- He was working from 14:00 – 00:00.

- The thought had not occurred to him to book the time off for such a momentous day.

- He had a lie-in (I felt this was harsh, he only got in at 4:30am).

- He bought Mummy some chocolates and prosecco (although she didn't complain when she was guzzling either of these).

- He admitted said chocolates and prosecco were just from the Mother's Day stand in Sainsbury's.

- He also admitted that they were a bit "standard".

- He treated Nanny to lunch yesterday. Mummy had to make herself some Supernoodles.

- He did not make a home-made card with my footprint on, with a witty caption (I was quite glad of this, he would have fecked it up anyway).

- He obviously had no appreciation of how Mummy will only get one first Mother's Day.

- She ran out of errors at this point and cried.

Poor Mummy. To make her feel extra special, I made sure I gave her one of my proper gummy smiles whilst I violently pooed all over my cute outfit. I know how to treat her right.

In Daddy's defence, he did write her two lovely cards: one from me, and one from him. Although both were obviously from the Sainsbury's stand.

In spite of the above, we did have a lovely time over at Grandma and Grandad's. Dummy battle with Grandma continues to rage on. I am winning. I heard Grandad say, 'She is very edible though, isn't she?'

I knew he was beginning to crack.

Month 3:

Out and about

13th March

Mummy left me with Daddy again this evening. I'm worried she's not that committed to me. Twice in two months is quite extravagant, I feel.

She went out for a meal with her friends, and left a bottle of milk for me, but she needn't have bothered. I was having none of it.

I was absolutely starving, though, so I decided to scream and scream and scream. Daddy was very panicked and obviously felt in quite a quandary: put up with a crying baby and let Mummy have a good time, or call her and get her to come home from her meal and end the auditory assault on his ears. After an eternity of fifteen minutes, he decided upon the latter, and Mummy rushed to the rescue and whapped her boob out for me. Honestly, there's nothing quite so good as fresh, body-temperature milk when you're starving because you haven't fed in a whole hour and a half. Yum!

Mummy seemed a little less than happy at having been called home, and kept saying to me that I'd taken a bottle before. As if! I would definitely remember imbibing from such a vessel and even in my younger days, surely I wouldn't have been so foolhardy?

14th March

Jesus, there seems to be a lot of days when we're meant to celebrate Mummy. It's her 32nd birthday today, and luckily Daddy made a much better job, after the detailed feedback on Mother's Day (although still no home-made card – some people never learn).

After a lot of rustling of paper this morning, Mummy and I went to Rhythm Time with Sophie and trendy Jasper. I don't know where his mummy buys his clothes, but he always looks amazing. Sophie and I decided it would be funny to take it in turns to cry during today's class. Andrea wasn't there so it just didn't have the same appeal. We made sure that our mummies were unable to have a secretive chat during any of the class by alternately crying during songs and demanding to be fed.

It's quite funny seeing how long they'll stick our crying out by looking sheepish and mouthing an over-exaggerated "sorry" to the other mums before admitting defeat, taking us to the back of the room, and attempting to feed us.

After class, Mummy, Daddy and I went for a birthday meal in Zizzi's. They were hoping to re-enact their pre-baby lives at their favourite restaurant, and even ordered the usual food, with the ridiculous aim of being able to eat it hot, and at the same time as each other. Mummy hadn't factored in that I too wanted to celebrate with them. By feeding. Non-stop.

When I say non-stop, I did break off to do what I believe is known as a poonami. What made it better was that because Daddy was trying to be kind to Mummy, he offered to change me. It took him a whole twenty minutes, as it required two outfit changes (I pooed all over some of the new clothes, whilst Daddy was dithering with the first pooey set).

Mummy was slightly perplexed that Daddy put all of the offending poo clothes into the same bag, rather than separating them on the basis of poo-coverage. This feedback was not met enthusiastically by Daddy.

After a tense car ride home, I fed again. I then vommed all over Mummy, and managed to soak her completely down to her underwear, then I fed again, and went to sleep. Mummy said it was normally her own vomit she got covered in on her birthday, and lamented the changing times.

I think she had a great day.

16th March

I've nailed it! I can hit the dangly objects on the Sensory Mat of Doom, pretty much every time, with my left hand. Maybe I am a genius? Next step, perfecting the right hand.

In other good news, my feeding has got a bit better since my snip last week. I like feeding off the left side better. Mummy reckons it's because it's closer to her heart. Ha, the loser! I just like it because, unlike the right side, I don't drown in milk so much when I feed from it. Mummy seems happier with the feeding, too. With this and the joy of the object-bashing success, she was beginning to get a little bit complacent, like she was cracking the whole parenting lark, so I've decided to mix it up a bit.

Most evenings, Daddy will cook, and I can tell when they're about to eat, because there's a strange pinging sound from inside the kitchen. This is the cue for me to begin the old root-and-nuzzle routine, just in time for Daddy to present Mummy with her tea. This way, she has to feed me first, or risk a teatime of crying and screaming, gulping down her food, and ending up with indigestion. Either way, it's a win-win for me.

Oddly, though, this strategy seems to irk Daddy more than Mummy. She is frustratingly unfazed and just opts to eat her food after I'm done. She doesn't seem to mind it cold.

Daddy, though, gets very frustrated and says, 'We're definitely not having another one.'

I think he must be referring to a hot meal that they can eat together... Which is very true.

19th March

Finding it really difficult to be held at the moment. I just feel so restrained when Mummy tries to cuddle me towards her. I can't see anything that's going on, which is very frustrating. Anything could be happening, and I'd miss it, because I'm looking at Mummy's t-shirt. Or worse, I'm facing over her shoulder and feel a bit sick from the backwards motion.

She finally got the hint today, when I screamed continuously as she shifted me about, until she hooked me under my legs and faced me outwards. Ah, the relief. To make sure she got the message, I made her hold me like that for over an hour, and any time she tried to move me, I whacked out the waterworks till she moved me back.

If anything, she should be grateful. This is a great workout for those flabby bingo wings of hers.

20th March

Met up with the dashing James again today. We had matching M&S knitted jackets with ears on, so obviously our grandparents have the same exceptional taste in shops and clothes. We also both have mummies who think taking your baby to a pub and drinking wine at lunchtime is acceptable, so maybe we are destined to be together, consoling each other over their impending alcoholism.

James slept for most of our date, which I considered a little rude, although apparently he's not sleeping very well at night, so I'll let him off. And it did mean I got lovely cuddles with his mummy, Katy, who kept telling me how cute and gorgeous I was, and how she was jealous of how much hair I had. She has loads herself, so I'm not sure why she was jealous, but she seemed to know what she was doing, and kept me facing outwards the whole time, so I could look around the pub. Mummy calls it being nosy. I see it as taking an interest in my ever-changing world.

Mummy and Katy were discussing their lack of sleep and James' and my apparent fussiness, and whether it was due to a growth spurt, a "wonder-weeks leap", or some other nonsense. (Mummy is too tight to have bought the actual Wonder Weeks app so just uses Katy's and knocks a couple of days off!) They decided upon a combination of both, after a lot of debate. Fools. I'm not leaping anywhere, and I'm constantly growing because I'm a baby. I just like getting my own way, and winding Mummy up is possibly my most favourite of pastimes.

23rd March

Today, I've been to heaven and back. I might complain about her at times, but I do love my mummy. Particularly when she massages me.

We went to NCT Hannah's house. She actually goes to a baby massage course, but because my mummy is (yet again) too tight to pay for it, Hannah said she would show Mummy and the other mummies (there were a lot of mummies there, it was confusing) what to do.

I wasn't convinced at first, as Mummy stripped me off in front of everyone (she's always doing that without a thought for my dignity), but then she oiled up her hands and started massaging my legs, and it was beyond delightful. Tainted only somewhat by her tuneless singing, the massage was glorious. It was that glorious, I may have pooed everywhere.

At least I managed to poo on the mat; unlike Jasper, who might have super-trendy clothes, but still vommed and pooed everywhere within a minute. As gross as it was, it was actually rather impressive, and something I'm going to attempt in the next few days.

I'm beginning to struggle again to feed. It takes forever. And whilst I do enjoy the time with Mummy, it means I can't practise hitting the objects on the playmat as much as I would like. The playmat that I love so much. She says I didn't used to like the playmat, but I don't think that's right. I've always thoroughly enjoyed being on there, and never once cried so much that Mummy wanted to rip off her own ears.

24th March

Even though I only saw most of them yesterday, today we met up with all the NCT babies. I was by far the best, as I managed to stay awake the longest. Whilst all the others were happily asleep, I was wide-eyed and bushy-tailed, and wanted to be bounced facing outwards when the food arrived. This meant Mummy and Daddy had to take it in turns so both their meals went cold. It was a genius move.

We then had to have a bloody photo with us all on. What a faff. I got punched in the head by Sophie, and I kicked two other babies in the head, and at least one of us was crying on every photo. I did manage to wangle myself next to James, which was a bonus, although I couldn't actually see him, as Mummy placed me down facing away from him, and I can't turn my head very easily, so I was stuck. I hope he didn't think I was ignoring him. I thought she was meant to be promoting this courtship.

27th March

Saw my Nanny today. She's bought me even more clothes, which are beautiful. She branched out and went to JoJo Maman Bebe. Think it must have been payday.

She loves seeing me so much. Daddy says I won't ever get to meet my Grandad Stuart, which is very sad. And my Nanny is very sad still that he isn't here, so I always do my best to cheer her up, and give her lots of lovely smiles.

We went for a lovely walk around the lake that my Grandad loved, and Nanny looked sad and happy all at the same time.

Then we had lunch in a pub, and I managed to expose Mummy's nipple to a seventeen-year-old waiter, which was hilarious. He didn't know where to look, and almost dropped the soup. Haha!

Refused the bottle they tried to give me. Obvs.

28th March

I have found the best game to play when feeding. I've given it the catchy title of "Clamp, pull and expose". It's quite self-explanatory, really. Firstly, I'll clamp my gums around Mummy's nipple, then pull my head back and try to look around the room, in case I'm missing anything, thus revealing Mummy's breasts for all to see. The bonus of this is that sometimes Mummy doesn't realise that I've exposed her to everyone, so it can be quite some time before she has to quickly scrabble to put them away, thus maximising the number of people who get an eyeful. I play it whenever I hear even the tiniest of noises, because I have serious FOMO. Who knows what might be going on while my head's turned... an old man sneezing; a fork being dropped; a door being shut. All these are valuable sensory experiences.

I find it helps pass the time when feeding as well, as currently I'm up to about forty minutes a time, which can get a little tedious for both Mummy and me.

1st April

I've had a very exciting couple of days indeed.

I've had my first sleepover at Grandma and Grandad's house. I should perhaps rephrase this to "stayover", as I didn't sleep very much last night. I was too giddy from my lovely day.

I saw lots of my favourite people and beamed at them all. Daddy was out with his friends, so Mummy took to me to the pub for a drink, and I got cuddled by everybody (and pretty much anybody, which was mildly concerning). Everyone said I was so cute and good. It was the best. I even had a little snooze!

Luckily, the snooze gave me the extra boost I needed to stay up for most of the night. It meant I could really examine the new room I was in, and savour the bright pink walls and lilac ceiling from Mummy's teenage years, whilst I fed numerous times.

Feeding from Mummy is still a bit tricky, actually, and both of us are getting very frustrated. I end up wriggling and squirming about, as I just can't get enough out quick enough. The word "formula" has been said a couple of times, but I'm not sure what this means.

Anyway, this morning my bleary-eyed parents (Mummy from the lack of sleep, Daddy from the beer) relinquished my care to my great-cousins, whilst they stole a nap. It was hilarious, as the great-cousins fight over who gets to hold me and play with me; so much so, they start "bagsying" the next cuddle. At one point, they even started timing how long each of them had held me for, like whoever held me the longest would become my favourite. I hardly have any say in the matter, which is a little annoying. And what's more, I probably won't remember them by tomorrow anyway.

We had an Easter party this afternoon, with even more of my family. I got loads of presents from my Grandma (the labels said Grandad too, but I'm pretty sure he didn't even know I was getting presents, let alone what they were), because it is Easter and I am almost three months old, which apparently is a big deal. To be fair, the fact I've managed to survive this long with Mummy and Daddy as my carers is quite an achievement.

3rd April

Today I have been to the beach. It was awful. Why anyone willingly goes is beyond me. It's windy, cold, and sand gets in your face. Horrendous.

I was also forced to get naked in a public car park in Whitby. Granted, I did the largest and squelchiest poo known to man, but I felt it could have been handled better. Anyway, three nappy bags, 115 wipes, and a new outfit later, and we were having a delightful fish and chips lunch when Mummy noticed my poo on Daddy's nose! Ha! He claimed at first it was curry sauce... good job he didn't taste-test it. Luckily, karma exists and as we left the restaurant and sauntered down the pier, Mummy, Grandma and Grandad all got shat on by a seagull, and it was Daddy's turn to laugh. A poo-themed day all round.

Refused a bottle again. My parents are not getting the message.

5th April

I've discovered the best thing... a bottle of milk. Some may call me fickle, but I really do love it. Especially when my Nanny gives it to me. I just want to keep drinking it, so much so that Daddy had to re-heat more milk three times, I guzzled so much.

May have overdone it, though, as then I vommed everywhere. Nanny and Daddy have decided not to tell Mummy that bit, as she gets a bit precious about her milk, for some reason. Keeps talking about feeling like a cow?!

7th April

Saw my Uncle Matt and Auntie Justine today. They are a lot of fun. My auntie loves to sit and read books with me (I say read... I just kind of gaze into space, but her voice sounds nice), whilst Uncle Matt enjoys waving toys in my face, and trying to get me to roll. I feel he sometimes wants me to be older than I am. But then I shoot him a smile and he's a sucker for it. He particularly enjoys it when I trump as well, and he says he's proud. Slightly odd, but I'll let it pass as his toy-waving is second to none.

Disappointingly, although I may have won many battles, my grandma has won the dummy war, and I'm addicted. Hooked. I just couldn't resist the silicone squidginess anymore. Man, it's like crack. Slightly annoyed at myself for being so stubborn for so long, and depriving myself of this prosthetic joy-giving teat.

10th April

I'd felt a bit down, considering I'd conceded on both the bottle and dummy front recently, so have found a new, and arguably much better, way to piss my parents off – waking in the middle of the night, and refusing to go back to sleep for quite some time.

I don't cry, because that's quite tiring to do for sustained periods of time. Instead, and it seems to have a similar effect, I babble. To myself. For a good two hours. Mummy tries to feed me, and con me into going back to sleep, but I'm wise to that trick. They try changing me; winding me; shoving the dummy in, but nothing will prevent me from gabbing away, and letting them hear my beautiful voice for as long as I deem necessary. Then, when I'm good and ready – and usually at this point at least one of them has started getting into something on Netflix which they then find hard to stop – I fall back to sleep. Genius.

11th April

Tomorrow is Mummy and Daddy's first wedding anniversary, and I will be three months old. At some point, I'm pretty sure I'll find this fact gross, but currently I'm too young.

Anyway, Mummy has been worrying all day about leaving me with Nanny tonight, as they are going out for a meal to celebrate. Pretty sure I'll be fine. Nanny is yet to bang my head on a fridge door, drop her phone on me, squirt milk and saline spray in my eyes, arrange for my tongue to be cut with blunt scissors, sit and watch someone jab me with needles, or publicly expose me in a car park in Whitby, so I'm confident she can cope watching me sleep for three hours.

Month 4:

Wind and midnight parties

12th April

So we celebrated the big three months with what seems to have become a monthly event; Mummy writing a hilarious do-it-yourself milestone card, and forcing me to pose next to it. Apparently, it's an update for all my adoring fans. This was after a photo session at the wedding venue where Mummy and Daddy got married, as Mummy thought it would be "so lovely" to go there one year on, and pose with their little bundle of joy. That is not what either of them are calling me in the middle of the night at the moment. Hypocrites.

What's worse, I also heard Mummy tell Niccy that sometimes she gets bored when it's just me and her during the day, and feels she's just doing the same thing over and over again.

Is she fecking kidding me? I'm the one who has to put up with the endless cycle between shitty tummy time, lying on my back swinging my limbs at inane plastic objects, "reading" a book with Mummy, and staring at epilepsy-inducing LEDs on various random toys. Not to mention the endless electronic music that spews out of every baby toy, which is only tolerable in comparison to Mummy's droning, tuneless renditions of nursery rhymes. I am literally on countdown until the next nap, so I can escape for a while. Sometimes, I pretend to be tired with a little eye-rub so I get put down early. I live for our trips out, so I can socialise with others.

14th April

I am in hell. Actual hell. A stomach-tightening, pressure-cylinder, gas-holding kind of hell. I just need to trump. A lot. I pride myself on not being much of a screamer, and certainly not without just cause. Especially in public, as I don't want people to think Mummy has it tough in any way.

But the last couple of days, I have been in absolute agony, and I've almost deafened myself with my screaming. To be fair, Mummy and Daddy have been really trying with gross gripe-water, endless hits of Infacol, and the most vigorous winding you've ever seen. But it takes a good seventy minutes of all of this before the glorious moment of gaseous release.

Needless to say, Daddy laughs every time. His pride is enhanced by the fact he is usually the one who has elicited the event, through a combination of over-the-shoulder-jigging and back-slapping, whilst also ssssshhhhing me to try and calm me down. It doesn't.

17th April

In my short time on this planet, I have learnt there are two groups of people: those who quite enjoy their own company and thus saunter through life, seeing people when it's convenient but never rushing or causing undue stress, and those who need to be around people constantly and cram as much into one day as possible, even to the detriment of enjoying what they are currently doing. You can guess which category Mummy falls into.

As if Rhythm Time wasn't enough (we've moved to a new one now, which is closer, but means no more Andrea – devo'ed), we now have swimming just forty-five minutes later. With a thirty-minute car journey between the two.

So you can imagine that the rush did not facilitate a positive attitude towards my new pastime. Which I can confirm is a load of shite. Here's why:

1. You have to get wrestled into an excessively tight costume. Mummy brought the wrong size, so "muffin top" does not begin to describe the rolls of fat that exude above and below this garment of torture.

2. You are in a vivarium with echoey walls, and it is almost as humid as the post-natal ward, bringing back terrible memories of realising just how inept my mummy was.

3. There are other babies there. Who also hate swimming. Except Jake, who's a right tosser of a show-off, and smiles the whole time. His costume seems to fit, so maybe that explains it.

4. The swimming teacher is THE most patronising woman ever. I know you're telling me to kick, Sandra, but I have limited control over my limbs in the open air, let alone when faced with the more viscous medium that is water.

5. It is cold. I don't care if they say it's warmer on the website. It's freezing.

6. There isn't a 6, as 1-5 are surely enough to realise swimming is a bunch of crap.

Hence my screaming so much that I had to be taken out. The best thing about it was watching Mummy awkwardly trying to sing the welcome song when she'd never heard it before. Worst thing: Sandra gave us another free taster session, because she said I didn't actually do anything. I did: I froze my non-existent breasts off, and cried.

18th April

I am a ledge. I don't want to blow my own trumpet, but I'm very advanced. Rolled over today. By myself. Obviously didn't let Mummy catch it on camera, because no one likes a show-off, but God I'm good.

19th April

Wow, today has been hot. And ever since one of the NCT mummies said 'Cold babies cry, hot babies die' at our meet-up today, Mummy has been unbearable. As a biology teacher, you would think she would have a little sense of perspective, and realise that as a species we wouldn't have survived for very long if all babies died when the temperature exceeded 23 degrees Celsius. Plus, other babies live in hotter conditions, and by my age are probably tending their own cow herds, and milking them, so I think I'll be OK.

Anyway, I'm now half-smothered in sun-cream, sat in a ridiculous frilly pink hat, and Mummy's frantically trying to make breast-milk ice lollies because she saw it on Pinterest, and obviously they're the only way I'll survive these arid conditions.

Even so, she was happy enough to leave me tonight to go out for a meal for Uncle Matt's birthday. Can't be that worried, can ya, Mummy?

22nd April

Considering Mummy is always stopping Daddy from buying new golf tops on eBay, because she's on maternity pay, we seem to go on lots of little breaks away, and eat out at pubs rather frequently. I'm not going to say anything, though, in case I am subjected to one of her eye-rolls, which are usually reserved for behind Daddy's back. Oh, and the fact I can't actually talk.

Anyway, we've been away for Uncle Matt's birthday and, as per usual, I was the star of the show. Apart from when I got bad wind again, and started screaming for thirty-minute periods pre-explosive trump, every couple of hours. Including through the night.

It was very hot again, so obviously Mummy worried endlessly about that. And we were away from home, so Daddy worried endlessly about my sleep and napping. Which I find slightly ironic, as it's Mummy who is up with me if I wake. But heyho.

At least they received some really helpful pieces of advice from my Great Uncle Bulgaria (he's called Julian, but thinks this is an excellent joke name), such as: 'We never had a monitor in my day, just shut the door and went back in the morning,' and, 'You don't need to entertain them all day, every day.' Also, 'I wouldn't touch a dirty nappy.' By the shaking of my

Great Auntie JoJo's head, I think he is either: a) telling the truth and she is still mega pissed off about it or b) lying, and actually he was as anxious as the rest of them.

23rd April

Because we need an extra class in our already busy lives, today we started Exercise with Baby. What I have determined so far is that I don't actually have to do any exercise; Mummy does some very low impact moves, but mainly tries to whisper to her friends and very occasionally picks me up and throws me about a bit to a nursery rhyme or pop song, in a bid to include me in this jaunt.

Luckily, Sophie and Jasper are there to keep me entertained. Sophie screamed all the way through it today, so I'll return the favour next week. Jasper says he'll take the week after. We find it only takes one of us to be a bit of a knob to taint an experience for all three mothers. It makes sense that we take it in turns and let the others conserve their precious energy, or risk all of us being so tired that we accidentally sleep through the night.

24ᵗʰ April

Overheard Mummy saying she was hoping swimming might tire me out so that I'd sleep well. Error, my friend. Never declare your well-laid plans out loud.

Lost slightly less of my shit at swimming as I actually quite liked it this week – mainly because Mummy had borrowed a new swimming costume so there wasn't constant squeezing on all of my internal organs. And I further complied with a three-hour nap post-swimming, which was, as you might expect, glorious.

Mummy "got loads done" in this time, and had a nap herself, which I feel is only fair, as now I am ready and raring to go for tonight...

25th April

As I had planned, and Mummy had not, I decided to try out a little 2am party, and man it was fun. I basically just stayed awake for an hour or so. For no reason. And because I'm still in their room, Mummy had to be awake too, as I made enough noise to ensure sleep could not be facilitated, but not enough to warrant any action. Apart from turning Evan the dream sheep back on every twenty minutes, and the desperate attempts to make me sleepy with milk, which I happily took, and then vomited over myself. Only a bit, though.

Worryingly, whereas a couple of months ago this would have triggered a full kit change, this time I remained in my milky-sick clothes. Mummy's standards have clearly dropped, but hopefully not as low for me as they have for herself, given she can't quite remember the last time she washed her bra.

27th April

As each week goes by, I learn another character-flaw of Mummy's. Today, I have discovered that she has the artistic capability of a wombat (I've heard they're terrible at art), and is less decisive than MPs voting on Brexit.

We went plate-painting, with the aim of making a Father's Day gift for Daddy. Obviously, this was organised by someone else; as already established, Mummy barely has the foresight to know when to wash her bras, let alone create a present two months in advance.

Anyway, she turned a relatively simple process into several huge decisions:

- What colour should my name be written in? She doesn't want it to be too girly, as she doesn't believe in pushing gender stereotypes on children. But equally, she really liked the purple.

- Should it be a footprint, or a handprint? Footprints are easier, handprints are cuter. Plus, this will be a life-long memory, and she has already forgotten to do the hand and footprint casts she got bought when I was a new-born.

- Should it be fifteen weeks or three months written on the plate? Three months looks like you've not been slowly counting each day, but equally it isn't as factually correct.

- What prints should she use? Dinosaurs so that I don't conform to gender stereotype, or bees because they're cute?

The list goes on. Needless to say, she fecked it all, as she didn't know when to stop, kept adding bits, and it now looks like I actually did do it myself.

Furthermore, I can categorically guarantee Daddy will not give a shit. If it isn't a golf top from eBay, it won't cut it.

1st May

Another unnecessarily jam-packed day filled with Rhythm Time and swimming, made even more rushed by the fact it was fancy dress day at Rhythm Time.

Now, my mummy might not excel at many things, but her dedication to a fancy dress competition can never be called into question. And, to be fair, I looked pretty epic as Harry Potter. I mean, I was wearing a bin bag as a cloak, and glasses from a child's medical kit wrapped in bin bags, but that aside, I was bloody cute. She even drew a scar on my forehead in eyeliner, but then promptly removed it as she was scared of the mummy-judgement, so she disappointed me somewhat in that respect. And then disappointment remained a theme throughout the day...

Just as I thought swimming was getting better, Mummy tries to fecking drown me. I kid you not, she full on dunked me for, like, ten minutes. Apparently, it was actually three seconds, but whatever. I could have died. Then she looked all concerned when she finally dragged me to the surface. If you're that worried, don't frigging do it!

4th May

Since I enjoyed my middle-of-the-night party so much last week, I've been continuing it ever since. At first, I just really enjoyed winding Mummy and Daddy up, but I think I'm addicted to it now. And it's been getting longer and longer. Even Evan, with his dulcet tones and glowing red body, can't lull me back to slumber. And I don't even make up for it in the day. But, if you can't do it when you're young...

Anyway, after complaining about "not having more than four hours' unbroken sleep since she was born", Mummy asked Daddy to have me for the night. At this point, I did feel like pointing out that I had slept for longer a while ago, but she insisted on setting her alarm to check I was still alive, so more fool her.

Anyway, poor, brave, valiant Daddy stepped up after my 23:30 feed. Mummy gleefully skipped off to the spare bedroom, and Daddy set about rocking and sssshhing me in the vain hope I would go to sleep. How deluded he was.

Obviously, I didn't fall asleep. And I kept letting out the odd yelp and moan every so often, combined with a lot of rustling, and a few babbles. I did this for maybe two hours, but knew I'd probably pushed it far enough when the following happened:

- Daddy broke the drawer off my nursery changing

table because it wouldn't fecking shut.

- He proclaimed, 'If my life was a book, this chapter would be called "This is wank".'

- Followed by, 'Why am I even here?' I think this was more the incredulous realisation that some people actually choose to have a second child (Uncle Rhys is older than him), rather than a profound question into the meaning of life.

At this point, Mummy came in and fed me, and we all slept for three-and-a-half hours. Didn't want Mummy to reach that magic four.

7th May

Another Monday, another Exercise with Baby class, where Mummy switches between naughtily chatting to her friends when the instructor isn't looking, to pretending to work really hard on her pelvic floor when she is. Mummy is also now worried she has abdominal separation, so has vowed to do more exercises at home. This was said in the same tone as when she vowed not to drink in the week, and to reduce her Victoria Sponge cake intake, so I have little faith in any abdominal gap closure.

Jasper maintained his side of the deal and screamed throughout the whole of the class, which was hilarious, whilst Sophie and I cheered him on.

In bigger news, I giggled today. And, I kid you not, Mummy started crying. Jesus, it's easy to get her going. I mean, it was possibly the most joyous sound the human race has ever heard, but still. What she doesn't know is that I was laughing at the fact she's giving up lettuce and onions in a bid to reduce my wind and improve my sleep, as she's read somewhere that this will work. She will literally believe anything she is told.

Mummy's reading about napping and sleeping (following more early-morning parties of mine) has also led to something new we are going to try. Apparently, she wants me to learn how to "self-settle". Whatever that means. And apparently we're starting soon! I hold very little hope.

8th May

Another day, another busy, class-filled Tuesday. Recently Mummy has taken to leaving the house an hour earlier than she needs to, driving around to get me to sleep and then parking up in the Rhythm Time car park and sitting by herself for 45 minutes in complete silence, just so I can nap.

On one level, I'm kind of impressed by her dedication to my napping schedule. On another, I'm annoyed that this gives her time to try and nap as well.

Today, just to prove that Mummy can't manipulate me in this way, I managed to resist falling asleep for a whole forty minutes by screaming constantly. It worked a treat as it meant I only slept for twenty minutes, and I was really grouchy for the whole of the class. Result.

9th May

So "self-settling" is a piece of piss. Not quite sure why anyone has a problem with it. You basically get to left to your own devices at nap time, get to slowly wind down, and drift off into a peaceful sleep without someone sssshhhhing you, or singing in their terrible voice at you, or having their elbow dig into you, or wake you up as they "carefully" place you into the cot. They should have done this from the start. Not sure what all the fuss was about.

However, if they even contemplate doing this at bedtime, I will unleash an almighty rage. There's no way I could ever fall asleep without boob, and Mummy's cuddles. The way Mummy looks at me adoringly at bedtime, I'm pretty confident she would never do this to me. In fact, I don't think she'd ever do anything to upset me ever. She's a good'un, to be honest. I think I'm really beginning to like her.

11th May

Mummy is THE WORST. And Daddy isn't much better. Yesterday they willingly delivered me to a pain worse than death at the doctor's surgery.

I had a vague sense of familiarity as we entered, but couldn't quite place why I suddenly felt so uneasy. Then I saw her: the pain-inducing sadist and tyrant of babies. Nurse Debra. Armed with three feck-off massive needles and the same drops of poison she forced upon me last time. Man, I hate her. She tried to smile at me and say how much I'd grown. Yeh, course I have, Debra, you moron. I'm a baby, that's pretty much all I do.

I saw through her façade and, sure enough, she jabbed me over and over again. And Mummy just kept whacking a boob in my face and telling me it would be alright. Liar.

What's worse, today she keeps touching the lumps on my leg, where Debra the Tyrant wounded me, and wondering why I scream out in pain. She thinks it's because I'm teething. It took half a day of screaming every time she touched me there for her to realise. There's no way teething can be this bad.

Month 5:

Re-attachment (of my tongue)

12th May

Unfortunately, I can confirm the updates are a monthly thing, and when asked how long these would continue (Daddy is not a fan of the monthly photo shoot, either), Mummy replied belligerently, 'Till she's eighteen.'

A couple of worrying things have happened recently that I need to keep an eye one:

- Mummy and Daddy have been taking me to the local pub, a lot. At least once a week. I feel this is excessive. Need to take some action.

- Mummy won't stop staring into my mouth all the time. I don't know what she's looking for, but it makes me nervous.

On the plus side, my late-night parties have now just become the norm, and Mummy doesn't even bat an eyelid when I'm awake for 2.5-3 hours in the night. I have to say, her optimism each night is to be admired. Without fail, she will refuse to use her phone for the first hour, so as not to wake herself fully up; ironically, she had read about this online, in the middle of the night, on her phone. However, she is clearly already awake. Then temptation takes over, and she ends up reading parenting forums on sleep, or Facebook posts on sleep, or Instagram posts on sleep, and gets more and more bamboozled by information, until she gets confused, and eventually whacks a boob in my mouth again, reads her book, and waits for me to drift off.

15th May

So it turns out all the late-night reading has been used to review and subsequently purchase a sleep aid; a McHummy. Apparently, this will cause me to sleep soundly through the night, and return to sleep after feeding without even a moment of alertness. Try your best, McHummy, try your best.

In other news, today Auntie Justine and Uncle Matt told Mummy I'm getting a cousin. I'm not sure what that is. Perhaps a different sleep aid, as Mummy did chuckle, "Get your sleep whilst you can," in between her tears of joy.

16th May

Oh my god, a McHummy is the most ANNOYING thing ever made. I feel like promising to sleep through every night, if they take it away. And I can't get the fecking thing to shut up. It makes this endless tinny, beating sound, and as soon as I think it's stopped and I can wriggle down to get comfy, *whooosh, whoosh, whoosh*, it's on again. Bring back Evan! At least he only lasted twenty minutes.

19th May

I went to a birthday party today. Not been to many, and it just seemed to be a lot of adults gathered in a hall, eating food and watching children run mindlessly about. Edie was there, who still couldn't give less of a shit about me if she tried, and is much more interested in someone called Lily, who is just the bees knees, it appears. Whatever.

Anyway, I decided I was way too mature for them and screamed so that Daddy would take me for a walk. My daddy may have a number of flaws (or so Mummy says, although it always seems to boil down to his golfing habits), but if there's one thing he is good at, it's being a stickler for naps.

Not much of a socialite anyway, Daddy saw his opportunity to escape, and said he'd be back shortly, after a quick walk to get me to sleep. Think again, Father, think again. Eighty-five minutes later, and I still wasn't asleep, because the fool had put the fecking McHummy in the pram, and it wouldn't shut up. God, I hate it. I don't care if Jessica from Wiltshire recommended it on the website, it is the devil's spawn and it needs to go.

22nd May

Mummy had a job interview today at her school, for a promotion. Which is fine. I was completely OK with it, until she started banging on about the fact she wanted to be a positive role model for me, and prove women can do anything, and blah, blah, blah. Shut up, you pleb. I know we can; I'm only four months old and I can roll, giggle, and pretty much nudge my dummy back into my mouth by myself if it's close enough, and I really focus on it. That's independence and feminist strength, right there.

We then went to the pub to celebrate the fact she went to the interview (literally any excuse, I knew I should be worried - she doesn't even know if she's got the job yet), and I had this shooting pain in mouth. Jesus, it was unbearable. It felt like it took over the whole of my face, and was just agony. Mummy and Daddy at least had the decency to leave their half-finished drinks and sweep me back home for a double hit of pain relief, which made it feel better. Really hoping it was a one-off... although the Nurofen was quite delicious.

26th May

Temporarily thought I'd been made motherless last night as, after feeding me to sleep, I didn't see Mummy for at least twelve hours, and she wasn't there when I woke up in the morning. I think she may have left me, but I can't be sure. This is probably because I slept through the night, for the first time ever. The main reason being Daddy forgot to turn on the McHummy, so I could actually get some bloody peace and quiet.

I don't know what Mummy did whilst missing, but I'm pretty confident it was not good for her health, as today she's looking very haggard (quite the feat when she already looks like death most of the time) and is not eating with the same gusto as normal. I felt a bit sorry for her, and decided to feed more often, just to let her know I care.

I thought she would be happier that I'd slept through, but apparently not. Kept banging on about "the one night..." Don't worry, Mummy, it will only be for one night, because you'll no doubt remember to turn that knob of a McHummy back on tonight.

29th May

I really am perplexed at the exceptionally low standards my mummy has in terms of what she finds impressive. Today, whilst in the epic Jumparoo, she caught me rolling the ball on it, and you would have thought I'd won a Nobel prize. Now, to be fair, it is something I've been practising for some time, and I have absolutely nailed it, but seriously... I don't think it warranted the phone call to Daddy at 9am. Slow news day, obviously.

In more interesting news, we went to a new class called Baby Sensory. Some of the NCT mummies had been banging on about how good it was and, not one to be left out for fear of everyone suddenly rejecting her on her lack of sensory-ness, Mummy signed up quick-sharp.

To be fair, it was actually very good, and I would probably give it a score of around 7.5/10. This was in spite of some poor, very public changing facilities, which I thought I'd let Mummy try out as soon as we got there. Just to settle her nerves. Sometimes I feel she doesn't challenge herself enough, so I made my poo an extra leaky one, and squidged around in it so she needed to complete a full kit-change in three minutes before the class started. She failed and was then flustered throughout.

Karen, the lady who ran the class, was possibly even more engaging than Rhythm Time Andrea (although I feel guilty just thinking that), and there were musical instruments there; there were bubbles, and puppets, and a massive cloth with stars on, which I quite liked. There's a welcome song that is just divine, although I have to look at other mummies, as mine doesn't have a clue how to sing or sign it and ended up looking a bit of a tool. Bless her for trying, though. There was one downside; I didn't get a name sticker to suck on, like I do at Rhythm Time.

If the dizzying heights of rolling the ball on the Jumparoo and attending a new class weren't enough, I also learned that my tongue-tie has reattached, which is rather exciting, and explains why Mummy has been worryingly staring in my mouth recently, and also why I can't blow a raspberry. There was talk of a 'snip' again, and there was no confusion this time... they meant me, and they meant my frenulum, and I told Mummy (well, screamed) in no uncertain terms, that *that* will *not* be happening.

1st June

Whilst it is hard for me to admit this, I may have been a slight bit of a knobhead this morning. My teeth were hurting again (hopefully a two-off and nothing more) and I was grumpy, due to contemplating life with a permanently attached tongue and what happens to people that never learn to blow raspberries. Are they ostracised from social circles? Will I be allowed back to Baby Sensory? You know, the rational things to consider.

Mummy wanted to get me weighed, so rushed to Niccy's to take advantage of her most accurate of midwife scales, so I screamed all the way through that and shit all over my outfit. Twice. This was not what she had planned.

She had then envisaged a lovely walk to meet the NCT mummies, where I would drift peacefully into an easy slumber so she could chat freely with her paid-for friends. Again, did not happen. She put the bloody McHummy on (they are sticking with it, even though I am still up every night for at least two hours, trying to show them how much I hate it), and I just lost it. Every time Mummy tried to put me down in the pram, I just screamed more. In fact, it was the moment I reached anywhere near a horizontal position that I started to cry, so much so that I barely scraped the pram mattress with my bottom before being promptly heaved back up again with a 'sod this!' In the end, she had to carry me whilst pushing the cumbersome pram, and felt she had to explain to every living soul we met the reason why. Obviously, I didn't sleep.

Then I didn't sleep all the way through till after lunchtime, which ensured Mummy couldn't eat more than some toast. I could probably have gone to sleep, but by this point I was on one.

Anyway, after a little snooze on the way to my beloved James' house, I awoke fresh-faced and full of the joys of early summer. Guilt started to eat away at me, and I decided to bestow upon Mummy the greatest of all gifts as she tipped me backwards and tickled me: a belly laugh. And man, it felt good. Mummy felt good (well, I think she did, through the predictable stream of tears), Katy felt good, James most definitely took notice, and we ended the day on a high. Apart from me pooing on the car seat on the way home.

3rd June

Because I'd not gained quite as much weight as Mummy had thought I would (you'd think she'd have given up on predicting or planning anything by now but nope... slow learner...), she's decided to become a feeder. I feel like all I hear is the double-unclipping of her greying bra and the strap top she wears pretty much every day, before being unceremoniously tipped on my side and stuck on her breast. It's non-stop. But delicious, so I'm not complaining.

Mummy was also hoping the extra feeds might help with the sleep, but no. Mainly because they've still got the McHummy pounding away through the night. Desperation has meant they've considered every possible angle as to how to stop my middle-of-the-night parties and came up with the idea that maybe I need more space, so they've moved my cot bed into their room and put it at the end of their bed. It's mega comfy and gives so much more freedom. I enjoy it most at around 2am, for an hour or so.

Mummy is a weirdo and apparently misses me lying next to her, so now sleeps with her head at the bottom of the bed. She deserves every bloody wakeful hour she gets.

5th June

The tides have turned! I fricking love swimming! After a pretty uneventful Rhythm Time and an extra feed in between the classes (because Mummy's still feeding me up), I had the best time.

Now I'm in a more appropriately fitting costume, the pool is my oyster. I get pulled around by Mummy like I'm a little fish, albeit more like a basking shark, as I don't actually make any effort to move at all. Unlike that chump Jake, who's kicking all the bloody time. Why exert energy when you can get dragged by your mummy?

Even Sandra, who is mildly less annoying now, admires my ability to do absolutely nothing in the pool. Apart from vom due to the over-feeding. Which she then has to scoop up in a net. Ha!

8th June

Ever the philanthropist, today I hosted my first charity event in memory of my great-grandma, who I never met, but who sounds like a ledge. Mummy says she hit my great-grandad on the head with an umbrella once. Amazing.

Mummy went all out, and even baked a cake. I thought I was surprised at this culinary endeavour, until Grandma found out, and actually laughed in her face with disbelief. Along with Grandma, there were some of Mummy's friends, and some of our elderly neighbours, who regaled us with tales of leaving their babies to cry in the garden back in their day with only a cat net for protection Yes, Margaret, that might be the case, but back in your day, infant mortality rates were also quite a bit higher, weren't they?!

There were games, most of which were thoroughly enjoyable, like "Hook-a-duck" in a bucket. This mainly involved me face-planting the water and licking ducks. The one I wasn't so keen on was "Guess the weight of the baby" – which was me! The cheek! I was under the impression you didn't discuss a lady's weight, but apparently this courtesy does not extend to under-ones. Anyway, my weight had gone up by 4oz and, as usual, Mummy looked extraordinarily proud of herself. I don't know why; I would only have gained two if I'd kicked like she wanted me to at swimming.

9th June

Bloody hell, it's hot again. And Mummy is anxious about it again. And Daddy's playing golf again. And my teeth are giving me agony again.

In spite of her anxiety about the heat, and the fact I had been grizzly all morning because of my teeth, Mummy dosed me up on Nurofen, and we embarked on an adventure to a carnival. Edie was there, with Niccy. She stroked my foot. It was amazing. But then Lily came , and Edie left me. One day she will notice me, I just know it.

Anyway, it was too hot to sleep, although Mummy blamed it on the lack of McHummy (for feck's sake, they still haven't figured that one out), so I got grumpier and grumpier, and we had to leave. Not before Lily went missing for thirty seconds, and I thought I'd got rid of her forever, and Edie would be mine again, but no, she turned up next to an ice cream van. Bollocks.

11th June

Proving just how uncommitted Mummy is to any cause, today we sacked off Exercise with Baby (no great loss, I'll be honest), and we went to visit Daddy in work, with Mummy's friend Lauren and her two boys, Teddy and Bertie. Now, they are the masters of destruction. From the moment I met them, I knew they were going to teach me some valuable life lessons in the art of parental winding-up.

And they did not disappoint.

We arrived at Daddy's police station (think *Heartbeat*, not The Met) and kicked things off by running riot around the joint and knocking numerous items over, including a police bicycle. They moved things up a notch when sitting in the police car, despite Lauren's numerous warnings of 'Do. Not. Touch. A. Thing.' Bertie managed to set the siren off with his bum.

Finally, when eating lunch, they screamed until they got ice cream, then chose bubble gum flavour, and ended up spitting all of it out whilst loudly exclaiming, 'This is gross!'

Excellent work, lads. Noted.

Month 6:

Teething. And pooing. Obviously.

12th June

The day started with my monthly update photo. For payback, I pooed a real stinker that leaked all over my car seat, and out of the front of my vest. Then I promptly fell asleep so that when we arrived on the driveway, Mummy had to choose between two conflicting pieces of advice:

- Never wake a sleeping baby.
- Don't let them sit in their own shit for too long. (I may have re-phrased that.)

Now that I wake the moment the engine is turned off and hear the keys leave the ignition, Mummy really didn't have much choice except to sit in silence in the car, on the driveway, with the engine running, dodging bewildered looks from the neighbours, Googling 'how quickly does nappy rash develop', and breathing in the scent of my somewhat rancid faeces, whilst I slept soundly on. It was so warm and snug, in my own faecal matter, that I slept longer than usual as well. Bonus.

14th June

Had some intense-sit training with Daddy today, whilst Mummy nipped out. I feel this comes more from Daddy envisioning an easier life with me having the ability to sit, rather than stemming from his innate need to drive my development and achieve milestones. I admire him for this, though.

And not only am I pretty much nailing the sitting, and absolutely nailing and exceeding expectations on the four-month sleep regression, I've decided to take my rolling to the next level. I thought it would be quite poetic to combine the latter two, so now I'm ending my middle-of-the-night parties with some rolling around, and ending up snuggling down to sleep on my front. And holy shit! I did not realise how successful a combination this would be, as Mummy is literally clueless as to what she should do. The oracles that are the NHS and Lullaby Trust clearly state I need to sleep on my back till at least six months. But I am only five months and two days. So Mummy is actually rolling me back when I'm asleep, which of course wakes me up. Then I can do some more partying. It's amazing.

15th June

Tried out the front-sleeping again last night; it is so much better. I can get all snuggly in my blanket and face-plant the mattress, so it looks like no air could possibly be reaching my nasal passages. Not sure what all the fuss is about.

However, my joy was short-lived, as this morning I woke and, sweet Lord, I've never known pain like it. My gums and my teeth are on fire, and I'm drooling like a dog in a butcher's. I'm getting through around ten bibs a day, and am continually high on a combination of Nurofen and Calpol. Luckily, Mummy has found some awesome gel that she rubs on my gums. As ever, she is cautious not to break any rules when administering such a life-saving remedy, and gives me exactly a pea-sized amount, to ensure I don't overdose and enter some sort of teething-gel-induced coma. Daddy, on the other hand, is just desperate for the screaming to stop, and basically coats my dummy in it. And he definitely doesn't wait the fifteen-minute intervals he should.

The heady mix of drugs and gel does make it somewhat better, but it still niggles away. To show Mummy what it's like, I've decided to niggle away as well. All day. Without stopping. A problem shared, and all that.

17th June

Teeth have been on and off the last few days, but I've been a trooper, and only moaned for around 80% of the time. I woke for my middle-of-the-night party and didn't feel any pain. To celebrate the blessed relief, I tested the acoustics of the room for three hours, with some top-notch babbling. Fun times. Mummy seemed particularly grateful, and was joining in with her own choice selection of words.

Today, after two months of diligently keeping the secret of our plate-painting (it's been harder for Mummy than me, I'll be honest), we got to excitedly (again Mummy more than me) bestow Daddy with his Father's Day plate. It went down like a – I believe this is the correct term – "lead balloon".

To his credit, Daddy showed mild enthusiasm upon opening it, but it wasn't quite the joyous rapture Mummy had envisaged. And the more Mummy said, 'Do you like it? Do you really? Are you sure? Do you think it's too girly and too factually accurate?', the more Daddy's responses: 'Yeh.' 'Yes. It's great.' 'I really like the dinosaurs and bees,' failed to meet Mummy's expectations. Until Mummy ended it with, 'Tell your face that, then,' and marched off, muttering some unsavoury language.

The day improved when Nanny and Uncle Rhys came

round for a BBQ. Nanny was quite sad at the start (I think because of Grandad Stuart), but I, selflessly, put my teething troubles aside and did my utmost to cheer her up. Pulling at her butterfly necklace; pulling at her hair; trying to gouge her eyes out. The usual stuff. She loved it, and kept giving me big squeezes. Lovely.

Uncle Rhys had his glasses on, which scare the bejesus out of me, so needless to say, I refused to go near him. Nanny kept trying to make me, but I made sure that as soon as he got within twenty centimetres, I screamed in his face. That'll teach him for being visually impaired.

20th June

Today I went to a delightful little farm, where I got to see a wonderful range of fences: some light brown; some dark brown; some with moss on; some with lichen on; some with shiny spiky stuff. They were quite the sight. Mummy and Daddy kept making weird noises as we walked past different fences, which was embarrassing, so I ignored them, and kept trying to bash the wooden wonders.

We then went to the pub AGAIN. And, weirdly, it was the precise moment I realised my mouth was really sore. AGAIN. Daddy necked his pint, whilst Mummy was slightly more lady-like and just left her ¾-full glass with a dejected backwards glance as we set off home. It's their own fault for forgetting the wonder drugs. Which they obviously blamed each other for. All the way home.

22nd June

Sometimes I impress even myself, with my own ingenuity. Not only does perpetually trying to sleep on my front cause Mummy more anxiety than my gunked-up eye back in the early days (and thus even less sleep), but I realised today it also means that when your poo leaks, it comes out the front of your nappy, through your vest, through the sheet, and onto the mattress. What's even better is if your Mummy is an absolute plonker and hadn't realised that your mattress has a waterproof side, which she has obviously turned to the bottom of the cot.

Cue a huge panic about how to get poo out of a mattress. An hour of Googling and WhatsApping various mummy friends, a subsequent trip to B&M, and a Zoflora purchase later, we're back at home, and she's dabbing (for God's sake, not rubbing!) the mattress, whilst I bounce for joy in my Jumparoo. Great morning.

Teeth not great again; my gums are that bad, I feel like grabbing the teething gel and downing it in one. Because I'm physically incapable of that, I've taken to shoving anything and everything in mouth; ball pit balls are my current favourite, but I'll accept fists (anyone's), jewellery, noses, and mobile phones. Basically, whatever I can grab. Except that soft, ideal-for-gumming, BPA-free teething ring Mummy keeps handing to me, which tastes weird, and is way too clean.

23rd June

Went to a gin festival today. It was shite. Screamed. Pooed four times in an hour and a half. Came home.

24th June

After a thoroughly disappointing day yesterday (apart from a great poo rate), today has been marginally better. My teeth have eased up a bit, and I got to see the NCT babies at a barbecue. Not that I enjoyed any of the food. I just sat and salivated, whilst Mummy and Daddy tucked in. Tried a few unsuccessful swipes at a burnt, carcinogenic sausage, but settled for boob in the end.

Unfortunately, Mummy had dressed me in the most ridiculous clothing for a hot day. A polyester England football shirt and shorts. It was itchy and sweaty beyond belief, and Mummy didn't fare much better in her matching one. All the other girl babies were dressed in appropriate summer dresses, looking cute and feminine. I looked more like Wayne Rooney than his own children do. Especially with my gloriously podgy tummy straining against the cheap material.

I did manage to steal a number of other babies' toys and gum them to death, so that's always a winner. I really liked this teething ring that Sophie's mummy got her. It was ideal for gumming and really soft. Delightful. Her mummy obviously really knows her shit.

27th June

FML. My fecking teeth are just the worst. And I don't even have any yet. I've decided (and Mummy agrees) that I'd rather be toothless and give gummy smiles for the rest of my life than go through this anymore. It was that bad, I couldn't even enjoy Baby Sensory that much, and it was Lights week, which is normally just the best.

Slightly more enjoyable was the awkward moment when one of the mummies at Baby Sensory saw that I could sit virtually unaided. Now, she is one of those mummies that does not cope well with other babies doing stuff first. And my mummy, although innately competitive and exceptionally proud of me (she whispers it to me all the time), has literally no idea of how to respond to this. At one point, I even think she tried to shove me a bit when saying, 'Oh but she's still really wobbly,' to make the other mummy feel better. Well, I was having none of that. I sat proudly for pretty much the whole session. Just to prove that, yes, I am indeed exceptional and talented. And I kept looking at the other mummy, and smiling, to embed this point further.

30th June

I have a sneaky feeling that my mummy left me again last night. She was there for bedtime, but today she appears to have that slightly grey tinge that she had last time she left me. And she wasn't there first thing this morning. And she is drinking lots of water. I can't be certain, as I fancied a full night's sleep last night, so had a night-off from my parties. Typical, one might say; Mummy certainly does, and lots of other things besides.

In spite of her odd colour and excessive thirst, Mummy and I hosted a first aid course at our house today for some of the NCT people. Bad decision. Mummy is now even more anxious about absolutely everything that could ever go wrong with me, and immediately ordered three first aid kits (surely one would suffice?!) from the lady, at an astronomical fee. This cunning lady knew her audience and had put a deposit down on her next Caribbean holiday by the time she'd left the gaggle of terrified mothers at our house.

The day ended with some confusion over whether my dummies had been sterilised or not (a pointless task; I dip the tips in mud whenever Mummy isn't looking) and Daddy stating, 'You're not as sharp as you used to be.' From the immediate intake of breath, exaggerated glare, subsequent violent throw of the dummies into the steriliser, and aggressive pushing of buttons on the microwave, even I could tell Daddy would not be playing golf for the foreseeable.

1st July

It is hot today. Very hot. Yesterday's course has only heightened Mummy's fear of heat stroke, sunburn and any other potential sun-related ailment. As a solution, she has bought me a paddling pool. After the expense of the multiple over-priced first aid kits yesterday, I think she may have gone budget, and it's in the shape of a rather angry-looking yellow snail. But who cares? It's cool, wet, and my poo floated beautifully in it when Mummy took a "what are the chances?" risk of removing my nappy for a quick splash.

3rd July

Today I have excelled myself. I've beyond excelled myself, in fact, if that's even a thing?! I've known for some time that I have real flair for excrement. But I didn't know until an epic eight-poo day today just how talented I am. And it's not just the frequency that's impressive; it's the timing.

I managed to poo three times in the same car journey. And I've suddenly got quite averse to sitting in my own filth. Call it maturity, if you will. So as soon as I've lost my actual shit, I lose my proverbial shit. And scream. Relentlessly. So much so, not even a dummy will calm me down. This can only lead to one thing: an in-car change. My favourite of all changes.

The best one was in the layby just after the second roundabout on the main road. I particularly like this layby, as it is often frequented by lorry drivers who seem to quite happily piss wherever they want, leading to a pretty over-powering stench of strange-man urine. So Mummy has a selection of odours to make her gag, which I think is quite considerate of me. I also like the way Mummy has to balance the nappy bag on the seat just within reach so that, if I'm really on my game, I knock it just as she's putting faeces-smeared wipes in. Great. Anyway, I timed it all so that I also required a change in the corresponding layby on the opposite side of the road on the way home. Talk about artistic symmetry.

4th July

"What the feck?! Babies can have more than just milk?! Holy shit, what a game-changer! I'll definitely stop my middle-of-the-night parties and sleep through now. My mind is blown!!!!"

This is the reaction Mummy was hoping for after she gave me some baby rice today. She was sadly disappointed. The way she's been building up "solids" is beyond ridiculous. She was so excited and nervous, I'm surprised she didn't do eight poos.

The reality was, it just tasted like grainy, ever-so-slightly-more-viscous milk. And even with my limited scientific knowledge of solids and their properties, it most definitely was not solid. Not that I got too much, as Mummy only gave me two spoonfuls, as she'd read somewhere to start slow. Not that slow, you tool.

5th July

Another expectation v reality check for Mummy today. We went to the zoo with the NCT crew. Boring!

A load of comatosed animals that I can't see, because the glass is reflective and I'm in my pram, so every other bugger is taller than me and blocks my view. Waste of time.

Mummy attempted some baby rice again. Pathetic. However, I did manage to try something utterly delicious. Charcoal bark. Now, that definitely is solid. And yummy. And leaves a really lovely black stain around the mouth. Managed to grab it when Mummy was helping look after somebody else's baby and she left me to my own devices. What's even better is that Sophie saw me and copied. #inspirational. Our mummies were not quite so happy with our foraging attempts, and both made a "don't tell the daddies" pact.

In addition to inspiring those around me to consume inappropriate items, I also seemed to induce poonamis in three of the other babies. They were obviously very impressed with my five poos whilst at the zoo, and wanted to join in. Some may say I'm a natural leader. I would have to agree.

7th July

A big family party today. Everybody has been running around like headless chickens, whilst Daddy and I have just chilled in the garden. Tried a bit of carrot puree, which was alright. Not as good as the bark, though.

Grandma bought me a new outfit to wear, as it's her party. It was awful. And finally Mummy and I agree on something. Mummy had been trying to find ways to get me out of wearing the offending item, to no avail, so she put me in it, showed me to Grandma, then pretended I was too hot and I'd vommed on it – both of which were lies – but I went along with the ruse.

Grandma was trying to show me off to everyone and I just wasn't feeling it, so I got really grizzly, chewed my hand a bit so everybody thought I was teething, and made an early departure to bed. It just looked like a load of old people getting drunk.

8th July

Well, a turn up for the books: drunk old people are hilarious! I did go to bed, but then woke up about 10:30pm and was whingeing enough for Mummy and Daddy to bring me downstairs in the hope it would "tire me out". Abso-bloody no chance. I out-partied Daddy in the end.

The tunes were banging, and everybody wanted to hold me and tickle me. Every little thing I did was "so cute" and "so funny". I can't help but agree, I am both those things, and more. I didn't want it to end. I did almost get dropped by a lady called Anne, but Mummy didn't see, so all was well, and I quite liked the thrill of it.

I finally succumbed to sleep after I pooed on a man named Dave. He didn't seem overly pleased, so I took that as a sign it was time to leave them to try and get Anne home. I wasn't walking her.

I was that wired from my midnight rave, I woke nice and early to make the most of the day. Got passed around from pillar to post by all the relatives that emerged in a post-party haze throughout the morning. Then something awesome happened. I got to try broccoli.

It's so squidgy and tickly on my tongue. I got to grab it and shove it in my mouth, and also drink it from a spoon (true to form, Mummy couldn't decide between baby-led and puree, so opted for both). Amazing. And even better... it led to a momentous occasion... my first poo in the bath.

I don't think Mummy and Daddy realise how very lucky they have been, because:

a) I'm almost six months old and I've never pooed in the bath before, not even a little one.

b) It was Grandma's bath. I'm familiar with the phrase "not on your own doorstep".

Mummy just pissed herself (maybe literally, as she has not been doing her pelvic floor exercises as she should), and Daddy got the bleach. Not for me, the bath. He wasn't that angry.

So, all in all, a fabulous weekend.

11th July

Another Wednesday; another Baby Sensory session; another pre-nap-on-the-way poo. I really like to time it for about ten minutes after the start of the car journey. That way, I know we are close enough to Morrisons; it's where all the VIBs go to get their nappies changed.

The facilities are to die for: clean hand-driers far enough away so Mummy doesn't set them off with her bum, and scare even more shit out of me, and a toilet for Mummy should she require one. Top-notch. I try and visit at least once a week. It's also quite fun as Mummy has to try and pretend she went into Morrison's to do something other than change my nappy. We normally end up browsing the magazines for an unconvincing fourteen seconds before she makes a dash for it.

Baby Sensory was pretty good again. Got to sit on an air bed during the interval, and there was a Teletubby puppet show. I'd give it 6/10. Then tried some butternut squash. Another 6/10. A mediocre day.

Month 7:

A holiday, teeth, and learning to crawl...

12th July

For once, I didn't mind the monthly photoshoot, as it ended a day that was all about celebrating me! Finally! I wore my best party dress for absolutely no reason other than I've survived six months in the care of utter wallies. That and the fact I wasn't going to get another chance to wear it, as it's a bit tight already and there's no parties on the imminent horizon.

Grandma and Mummy took me shopping, and we had a wonderful time. It started off well when I ate some sweet potato (pureed, of course – 8/10) and then got even better when Mummy let me gnaw on a pizza crust when we had our "ladies' lunch". I mean, I knew I was mature, but I literally don't know any other baby that gets to eat pizza crusts with potentially too much salt in them... delish.

Also met up with Mummy's friend and her baby Hamish, who just seemed so little and cute. He certainly doesn't get to eat pizza crusts yet. Made sure I showed off my sitting to him; tried to be inspirational.

A significant, and somewhat shocking, downside of the day was the lack of spending in M&S by Grandma. Normally, she is a sure-fire bet on getting me the cutest little set of clothes, but she didn't buy me a thing. Literally nothing. Must be a tight month on the final salary pension of a retired GP...

14th July

Tried some swede today. Gross. 2/10. Would not recommend.

I also wouldn't recommend getting any teeth, as I'm still suffering bouts of agony every so often. I feel like they're ripping through my gums – surely this is some form of torture? I keep hinting to Mummy that I want an IV of Nurofen, but to no avail.

I was that knackered from my teeth hurting so much, you'd think I'd want more sleep, but you'd be categorically wrong. They hurt less at night, so I had an extended midnight party to remind Mummy just how cute I can be when I'm not grumpy because of my teeth. She didn't seem to appreciate it. However, she still shot me the old adoring eyes when she fed me for the third time in three hours as she tried to force-milk me back to sleep, so I know she's still hooked.

15th July

This month, I am making some serious headway on the milestones... I've only gone and shaken a rattle for a prolonged period of time. I kid you not, it was very impressive. Although no tears from Mummy this time. I think she was too tired.

Mummy's taken to randomly running her fingers across my bottom gums, at least thirty times an hour, to see if any teeth have popped up. It's so fecking annoying. I'll just be going about my usual business and *swipe*, she's done it again, before I've had the chance to clamp my lips firmly shut. Not sure she's heard of a watched kettle. Plus, it tastes of antibac, which is gross. I'd rather take my chances with whatever microorganisms are colonising her fingers than have that taste in my mouth.

18th July

I knew today was going to be a good one when I finally felt my tooth break the surface. Oh, the joy! And it's so jaggedy, and feels so scratchy, I love it. And it looks like Mummy loves it too as she's still randomly running her fingers across it and looking proud every time she feels it. Anyone would think it was her who had been through weeks of agony.

The day got even better when I tried aubergine – a solid 8/10. Pretty confident this was the first aubergine Mummy had ever bought, so she's slightly hypocritical in expecting me to eat it, but it was delicious, so I didn't care. Not as delicious as formula, which Mummy let me try today too. Apparently, now that I'm six months old, I am suddenly old enough to have this specifically-made-for-babies liquid, even though some of my friends have been having it from day one. God knows what would have happened should I have had it this time last week.

And holy crap, that is some good shite! Way better than boob milk. Wish I could have just had this from the beginning. Mummy did not look quite so pleased as I gulped it down without breaking for air and demanded more.

20th July

Another day, another tooth popping through. I am literally the most advanced baby I know. Had a pretty quiet day, and then Mummy and Daddy started to act very suspiciously as it got closer to bedtime and beyond. I may only be six months and eight days old, but I know dodgy behaviour when I see it:

- They were happy. More than happy; I'd go as far as to say positively giddy.

- They smelt funny.

- They'd both washed their hair.

- They kept looking at each other as if they actually liked each other.

- Mummy wore a towel over her clothes to feed me.

- Mummy's heart was beating very fast, and she was mildly sweaty as she fed me to sleep. I say sleep, but I didn't actually go to sleep.

- They weren't there when Nanny got me out of bed thirty minutes after being put down, and still weren't there when I actually went to sleep four hours later.

I would say that they'd gone out for the evening together, but I highly doubt that. I'm pretty confident they hate each other, if the bickering is anything to go by.

21st July

After a late night with Nanny and Uncle Rhys, where I forced them to read endless stories and play endless games of peekaboo (suckers!), I slept through and woke nice and early to check Mummy and Daddy were OK.

They weren't.

They seemed a lot less giddy, and looked a bit more green. They still smelt funny, but not a good kind of funny. Needless to say, I decided to make them feel better by demanding to be held by no one else but them all day. And refusing to sleep on the hour's drive home, as they had planned. Instead, I had a moment of pure brilliance and pooed everywhere in the car seat. Even managed to leak some through the precautionary muslin (which Mummy now lines the car seat with, thinking she's being clever) so it soaked into that super absorbent, and nigh on impossible to remove and wash, car seat cover.

Then we were back on more familiar territory: a battle ensued as to who had drunk the most, and was therefore unable to complete the clean-up operation. Which is weird, as surely the more hydrated parent would be feeling capable to deal with this. Anyway, in the end, they reached a compromise and tackled the scene of devastation together, whilst retching. I managed to get a sock and one of my dummies to land in the mess as well, during their inept attempt to eradicate my faecal matter.

Finally arrived at my great-grandma and great-grandad's, only to find I had my own battle to fight. There was an intruder. An invader. I hated her.

Ella. Or, as I prefer to call her, the Beast. She is apparently Mummy's cousin's daughter, and she was bigger than me, quicker than me, could talk, and walk, the works. So I knew I had to bring my A-game.

I started by just staring at her. A non-blinking, soulless stare that would make even the largest of ogres quake. But the Beast just stared straight back. After this carried on for about five minutes (the onlookers at first found it funny, progressing to nervous laughing), I screamed in her face. She screamed in my face.

I shot Great-Grandma my cutest smile, complete with my precious, budding teeth. The Beast smiled with a full set of pearly whites.

I tried to pass Great-Grandma a ball, the Beast went over and hugged her.

Sometimes you have to admit defeat, so I just cuddled Mummy and took comfort in the fact that, unbeknownst to her, I was squeezing out my remaining poo onto her jeans as, in their mockery of a car-nappy-change, they hadn't put my nappy on properly.

22nd July

Today has been a funny old day; I'm now on my holidays, and apparently I've been on my first flight. Not that I would know, as I slept through most of it on Mummy, ensuring that she was penned in the whole time, and couldn't go to the toilet, for fear of waking me. Piece of piss, this flying malarkey. But not for Mummy.

What I do know is that it's bloody hot on my holidays. And I get to stay up late on my holidays. And I get to have four adults all to myself on my holidays: Mummy, Daddy, Nanny and Uncle Rhys. This is going to be fun.

23rd July

On my holidays, you get to go swimming. And the best thing about this swimming is the fact that Jake the tosser isn't there to show off how good he is, and I can do whatever I want. I get to jump in from the sides and be dunked all time, and I get this cool, inflatable yellow carriage that I make Uncle Rhys drag me around in for ages. It's awesome. He doesn't wear his glasses in the pool, so I'll actually let him near me.

What's even better about my holidays is that I don't have to tolerate any of Mummy's home-made purees but instead get the shop-bought pouches that I really love. And endless cucumber from the buffet. Winner.

25th July

Tried a banana today – minging. 1/10.

What's also minging is sand – literally the worst thing ever. Grainy and sticky, and generally horrendous. Not a fan, so obviously screamed.

A positive of the day was the fact that, after numerous weeks of trying, I've pretty much nailed the backwards crawl. By nailed, I mean I can do one knee and hand backwards in a coordinated motion, before I stop and sit again. Mummy and Daddy watch and encourage me endlessly, and call me a clever girl. I am not a fecking performing monkey, so I'm refusing to do any more crawling now.

28th July

Met an older man today. And whilst I'm obviously loyal to James, I don't think it's unreasonable to do a little holiday flirting. His name is Stavros, he's sixty-three years old, and he's a waiter. I smile at him endlessly during mealtimes. He loves it, and it means that I can throw as much food on the floor as I like, and he doesn't mind cleaning it up. What a legend.

What isn't a legend is herring. What a disgusting food. 0.5/10. I'd rather eat a hundred bananas. Not quite sure why Mummy thought I would like herring. Think she did it to piss Nanny and Daddy off, after they tried to sneak me ice-cream when she wasn't looking. Ever since the health visitor scared the shit out of her a while ago with tales of obesity, refined sugar addicts and rotting teeth, she is refusing to give me anything like that. Which is mildly hypocritical, given she takes sugar in her tea, eats endless cake and chocolate, and is averaging four plates a meal at the buffet, not including dessert.

29th July

So now I see why they said flying was shite. You're trapped in a metal box, in the air, with nothing but annoying people, and if some loud knobhead from the seat in front wakes you from your slumber with his ridiculously loud voice, you can't even sleep through it.

So you have to be passed from relative to relative in a lame bid to entertain you. I knew they had got desperate when their ten-minute rota had dwindled down to a quick ninety seconds before I was passed back to Mummy. What made it worse was Mummy constantly doing the old lift-and-sniff test to see if I had pooed, as it turns out sour cream Pringles smell exactly like breastfed-baby poo so every time someone popped and couldn't stop, Mummy thought I'd defecated.

The only saving grace was the wonder that is Freddie Firefly that Mummy had the foresight to buy especially for the flight. I'm normally loath to admit she has achieved any form of parental competence, but this deserves an exception. He has everything! He's squeaky (payback time for the knobhead in front), squidgy, rustly, and awesome to scrape your teeth over. He even has a little mirror on his wings.

31st July

Saw James today and, whilst he is certainly pastier than Stavros, he is definitely cuter, and can pull off a pair of dungarees like no one else. Only downside is his very scary daddy. He loves to terrorise me by trying to play peekaboo and passing me toys, and other unreasonable acts. He needs to cut it out if wants to be my father-in-law.

2nd August

Despite making it very clear that bananas are truly disgusting (screwing my face up and launching them as far as my underdeveloped motor skills will allow), Mummy seems determined for me to like them. I don't think she realises that this is not like the time she made herself like olives by eating them ten times, and just because they are a convenient snack and every other baby loves them, it does not mean I will. In fact, it makes it less likely that I'll like them, as I am not one to follow the crowd; I am one to lead.

This was exceptionally evident today, when we met up with the NCT babies, or as I now like to call them, my groupies. Because I've got teeth and can sit up and crawl backwards, I am obviously leading the way. Whilst I think this is something to show off to the world, Mummy is overly and unnecessarily conscious about it, and tries to play down my achievements for fear of upsetting other mummies. I had other plans. I decided to make sure everyone was watching, and then I crawled backwards into the circle, to make sure I was holding court, then did a big toothy grin, whilst sitting up nice and straight.

At this point, other mummies started to exclaim, 'Oh she can crawl/she has teeth/she can sit so well!'

Mummy said 'Yes, but she's basically a mute and never

babbles,' to which I said, 'Ba ba ba' as loud as I could.

Just to prove she's a liar and cannot be trusted. I refuse to hide my light under a bushel for anyone!

4th August

Daddy was missing today, and was playing "golf again". I'm not sure if this is a special version of golf or just what Mummy always says.

Being the eternal and completely unrealistic optimist that she is, Mummy had envisioned a wonderful day of mother-daughter bonding, whereby we would have just the most joyous of times sharing each other's company. What Mummy doesn't realise is that this is nigh on impossible for two sleep-deprived individuals; one who is a hormonal wreck, and one who is as fickle as the day is long.

The day did not start well for Mummy as, on our way to trusty Morrisons, I pooed all over the car seat – the precautionary muslin had (unbeknownst to Mummy) been removed by Daddy and not replaced, and I can assure you this did not go down well. After a full kit change (she should be grateful we got to see the treat that is that changing room), I pretty much screamed all the way round the shop, as Mummy kept trying to put me in the bloody buggy. Some may say this was an over-reaction, but I hate it in there; I just feel so trapped.

So, after walking round Morrisons with a baby in one hand, pushing a buggy with the other, whilst also trying to shop, Mummy exhaustedly placed me back in the car and realised she had stolen a bar of Galaxy and a pack of wipes. At which point, she sat in the car, cried, and decided to go back and pay for it at a later time. She refused to eat the chocolate as she thought that might somehow make the crime worse.

After washing and drying the car seat in quick-smart time, we headed over to Grandma's. And I may have pooed again. All over the car seat. Which Mummy had forgotten to put the precautionary muslin on, so she couldn't even blame Daddy. Cue more tears. And a lot of snot. From both of us.

Anyway, decided to up my game when we got to Grandma's. Partly as a nod to Mummy's dream for the day, but also to ensure Grandma thinks Mummy has an as easy life, and that I am absolutely delightful at all times. I giggled non-stop and found Mummy hilarious as she whacked out vigorous renditions of *The Grand Old Duke of York*, and all was well with the world.

7th August

Man, I love cucumber. It's just so full of watery goodness, and it's like a cool slice of heaven upon my gums. I also like the fact that Mummy doesn't like it (seriously, she'll eat herring but not cucumber?!) so has to pretend to eat it when I shove it in the general direction of her mouth. Ha!

Continuing to smash the milestones, as I can now wave and high-five. Mummy thinks I'm a genius. Really, I just copy what she is doing, but we don't need to dwell on that.

Really focusing on my crawling, but it's so fecking frustrating. I can get quite a good rocking motion when I'm on all fours, but then I'm not quite sure what to do: do I go hand-first, knee-first, or head-first? Head-first hasn't worked out that well for me, as I keep face-planting the carpet, so think I'll try knee-first tomorrow.

8th August

Tried strawberries today. They're weird, and I can't decide whether to give them a 1/10 or a 10/10. At first they make me shudder, but then I can't help going back for more. And I repeat this for the entire strawberry. Mummy can't stop laughing and taking photos of me when I eat them, which I think downgrades them to a 4/10, because I hate the invasion of privacy that accompanies them.

Saw James the beloved today, he's such a ledge. He was rocking a little sailor's hat, and he was really kind and let me pull it off his head about eighteen times. Not that he had much choice, as I'm way quicker than him, but still, I reckon he liked it, and loves me even more now.

Also went to an exercise class with Mummy in the evening, which got the old adrenaline pumping, and meant I was nowhere near ready for bed at seven. Or eight. Or nine. Or ten.

In this three-hour window of bonus awake time, I continued to practise my crawling. After yesterday ruling out the fact it's definitely not head-first, I tried knee-first as planned. No such luck. I just keep banging my knee into one of my arms, and then toppling over. Will try hand-first tomorrow.

11th August

Fecking nailed it!!!!!!!!! The world is officially my oyster, and I am on the move!

Turns out you kind of have to coordinate the movement of both arms and legs at once to crawl effectively. And bloody hell, I'm really good at it.

In other news, got to try some home-made flapjack today at Daddy's friend's house. I say "try" rather than "eat" as, after I'd stealthily procured it from the floor without anyone noticing, the maker of the flapjack said, 'Is she eating flapjack? That's got honey in it,' to which Mummy predictably leapt up in a panic. However, while she is fully aware that honey is the devil's sap, she equally did not want to appear rude or over-protective. In the end, her maternal instinct won, and she tried to secretly scrape it out of my mouth with no one looking. Her mission was unsuccessful as I screamed when she did it, highlighting just what was happening to all and sundry. Needless to say, we left rather quickly after that.

Month 8:

Crying my heart out

12th August

Argh! I should have waited till tomorrow to crack the crawling, as Mummy was able to bulk out her monthly update with it. Bollocks! However, I don't know how I ever managed to live without crawling – you can just do so much. Well, quite a bit. Until your mummy grabs you and prevents you from licking the fireplace tiles, or touching those very intriguing trios of holes in the wall.

14th August

A large contraption has appeared in my conservatory, courtesy of Grandma, and I am not convinced it is a good thing. On initial viewing, it seems to be quite the object of joy: glorious pastel colours, cute teddy faces stickered on, colourful playmats underfoot, and some random plastic shit that you can spin round and honk, but I just get an uneasy feeling whenever I go near it.

This may be due to the fact that Mummy keeps referring to it as a "jovial prison", and saying, 'Ooooooh, I'll be able to get so much done!'

I'm suspicious.

15th August

I bloody knew it; the contraption is a cage. To trap me in. So Mummy can attempt to do the housework she normally (and quite happily) neglects. I'm fricking outraged! Needless to say, I am yet to be locked in it for more than twenty-four seconds, as I just scream, and Mummy hasn't got the resolve to leave me to cry for any length of time. Mainly because I've worn her down with my continuing midnight parties, but also because she's soft.

Her attempts to get me to go in are pretty pathetic as well, and she clearly underestimates how intellectually superior I am. She thinks she can trick me into being distracted by starting off playing with toys with me, but then gradually sneaking away. Luckily, the door has a slight creak to it, so as soon as she attempts her escape and locks me in, *boom!* I'm onto her, and screaming ensues.

Met up with Mummy's friend Penny and her daughter Emilia today. She is quite the ledge. And hilarious. Although not particularly good at cuddles, as she seemed to think this was code for "strangle around the neck". She's staying over tonight, so I am hoping to entice her into one of my midnight parties.

16th August

Emilia did not oblige, and the loser slept through the night. She has seriously gone down in my estimation.

19th August

Had one of the best nights of my life last night. I think you had to be there to really appreciate it, but it was just so much fun, I've got to share it.

We were round at Great-Auntie Jo Jo's new house, and Daddy was away playing golf again. Mummy (having serious FOMO) had the bright/ridiculous idea that after putting me down to sleep at Great Auntie Jo Jo's, she would transfer me to the pram, walk me to Grandma and Grandad's, and then transfer me to the cot. What an absolute fool. I do not cope well with being in new places at bath time or bedtime so, despite my firing an initial warning against the idea with a poo in the bath, Mummy took no heed and continued with her exceptionally flawed plan.

After tossing and turning for ages, I awoke at 10pm, in the mood for a party. Admittedly, this was earlier than usual, but think I had caught a bit of FOMO off Mummy. Mummy saw her opportunity, and tried to put me in the pram so we could leave. Uhmmmmn... no. Nope-ity, nope, nope. Why would I want to be in a pram when I could be carried in the folds of Mummy's soft, snuggly bingo wings? So Mummy had to walk, carrying me whilst also pushing the pram, all the way, through a busy town centre at 10pm. God knows what people thought. She tried to dodge people by taking the back road for the last part of the journey, but ended up seeing three childless people she went to school with, which was awkward for them and her, but comedy gold for me.

When we arrived at Grandma and Grandad's, I was far from sleepy, after the invigorating late-night air, and decided to have a little play with my lovely grandma, who was more than willing, despite Mummy's mild protestations. It turned into a longer playtime as every time Mummy tried to put me to bed, I would just scream so she'd have to get me out. Managed to catch the end of *Match of the Day,* which was a bit of a bonus, as the green grass is just hypnotic.

This continued for an hour or so, until eventually Mummy, Grandma and Grandad decided to go to bed. I was far from done. Outraged by their fatigue, I screamed and screamed and screamed, and Mummy kept coming in and trying to shove a boob in my mouth, and I kept spitting milk out and scratching her.

Four hours later, after thirty minutes in Mummy's bed, trying to gouge her eyes out every time she closed them, I noticed fluid leaking from them. After I'd established it wasn't blood but just the salty tears of her exhausted sorrow, I laughed in her face and promptly fell asleep. If I knew I was upsetting her that much, I would have gone to sleep straight away. Some people just can't take a joke.

20th August

What the feck? My bastards of parents have actually grown some balls and started something ridiculous called "cry-it-out", or some shite like that. Apparently, my antics the other night were "the straw that broke the camel's back". Grandma didn't help my cause as she jumped on the bandwagon, saying that she didn't realise how bad I was, and how tired Mummy was, and that it was ridiculous. Not sure how pleased Mummy was about this, given it's been occurring for around four months and Grandma is always complaining about how tired she is, but heyho....

Anyway, bedtime came around; had a bath, weed in it, had a story with Daddy, milk from Mummy, the usual routine... and then she put me down AWAKE. And left the room.

At first, I thought she was just taking the piss, and would come back in with her goofy smile and snuggle me back to sleep, but no. She left me. And didn't come back in. Obviously, I screamed.

After five minutes, she came back in and I thought I'd cracked her, but she just rubbed my back, said, 'Goodnight, love you,' and fecked off again! I was incensed! She then left me for ten minutes and did the same. Then fifteen minutes. I was bloody fuming and just screamed throughout.

Now, I've always considered myself an over-achiever, but I seriously impressed myself with my performance. Two hours. Of constant screaming. Annoyingly, Mummy or Daddy kept coming back in every fifteen minutes (smelling a bit of wine, I noticed), which wound me up even more. In the end, I got one of those headaches you get from deafening yourself with your own screams, and felt into an exhausted slumber. Surely this is some form of torture.

22nd August

Screwed myself over the other night, as my exhausted slumber meant that when I woke for my feed, I was so tired I fell back to sleep straight away and didn't keep Mummy up, so they think it's been a success. And I did the same last night. And if I'm honest, I look a million dollars today because of it, and feel so refreshed. Mummy looks about a hundred dollars and has definitely upped the frequency of *The Grand Old Duke of York* recently, which is just the best.

Obviously, this has nothing to do with Cry-gate (as I have officially named it), but is entirely due to the fact that I have made a conscious decision to stop my extended midnight parties and focus on my mental and physical wellbeing.

24th August

Made two important discoveries today:

- If you're hungry, a good lick of the bottom of a shoe (preferably one which belongs to somebody you know, but that's not a prerequisite if you want to live a little more dangerously) takes the edge off it.

- If you want to get your Mummy's, or anyone's, attention, a quick little fake-cough coupled with a laugh works a treat every time.

27th August

Met up with James my beloved today. He was rocking some jeans. Sometimes I worry that because my mummy is so untrendy, he won't like me, but from the way he was watching me crawl today, I don't think I have anything to worry about. I mean, I was kind of showing off to him, but I wanted to check that he liked an independent, strong, fast-as-a-whippet woman. He was definitely very impressed.

28th August

I'm aware that often I berate my mummy quite a lot, and it is thoroughly earned. However, sometimes I have to hand it to her, she is absolutely hilarious. Today, we played a new game called Monkeys on the Bed, and once I got past the fact her voice is getting progressively more annoying with each nursery rhyme she sings, we had a whale of a time.

In summary, she bounces me up and down on the crappy spare room bed (it may be crappy, but it gives excellent lift), and pushes me over when the monkey falls out of the bed. Sweet lord, it's just the best. So much so, I made her do it for an hour. I'm a little concerned for her fitness levels, as she was quite the sweaty mess by the end. Maybe she needs to go back to Exercise with Baby again.

31st August

Daddy's playing golf again – again – and this time for the whole weekend, so it's just me and Mummy against the world. I had my initial reservations. But, to be fair, we've had quite a lovely day.

We went to a play place, and who should be there but Edie the Ledge. I immediately started to show her my crawling and how advanced I am now, and she was bringing me toys, and I could tell we were destined to be friends for life, but then who should turn up but fecking Lily! God, she's annoying. Edie instantly dropped the toy she was about to hand me (onto my foot, which was just rude), and ran off. I was gutted. And this was exacerbated by the fact that I was left to play with boring old Tilda (Lily's sister). She literally can't even sit. What am I meant to do with her?

I ditched her quickly, and set about crawling everywhere, much to Mummy's constant anxiety, given there were quite a lot of big boys running about and I was getting under their feet a lot. Unfazed by the endless stream of human traffic, I continued to crawl around the whole venue, to ensure Mummy had no time to eat any of her food, or talk to her friends.

We went on to meet the NCT Mums (so far, this weekend seems to be all about Mummy?!) and I ate some beef tagine (9/10, delicious but could have done with a bit more seasoning), and Mummy had a cheeky glass of prosecco. Naptime drifted and drifted, until I ended up with a danger nap. Interestingly, Mummy did not reveal this to Daddy, the Hitler-of-naps, when he rang at 8pm and I was still awake.

1st September

Yesterday pales into insignificance compared to today. We went to a beach. With Edie. With no Lily in sight. For the whole day. I don't think I've ever been to a beach before, as I would definitely remember somewhere that is packed full of such grainy deliciousness. It was amazing.

I managed to eat a considerable amount of sand before Mummy had to scrape it out of my mouth with her fingers, and try to distract me with my dummy. Which was an unwise move, as then I could just dip my dummy in the sand and eat it that way. Yummy.

And Harry, Edie's dog, was there, and kept licking me, and it was so funny. Edie and I napped together, we had a meal for two together, and bathed together. I may have ruined that slightly by pooing, which caused a mass exodus, and ended up with Edie crying at the sight of my floating faeces, but all in all, a most wonderful day.

2nd September

Ventured to a food festival today with the parentals and Uncle Matt and Auntie Justine, who is getting rather chubby. Nobody seems that bothered by her spiralling weight, but surely someone needs to say something. I try, but "ba ba ba" doesn't really deliver the hard-hitting message I'm aiming for.

When you're eight months old, a food festival is actually pretty shite. You can't really eat chilli halloumi fries with a side of wasabi, so apart from a quick feed in the park, and managing to expose Mummy to a few hundred people, it was boring. We went back home and had a roast dinner.

Now, always the optimist, Mummy had this idyllic image of how my first roast dinner would be perfect, and we'd all be sat round the table as a family, and it would be just Walton-esque great. Well, it tasted horrendous, so I rubbed some of it in my hair to make Uncle Matt laugh, and then refused to eat anything but a fruit pot. One day, Mummy will learn.

4th September

Mummy left me today in the more capable hands of Great Auntie Jo Jo, which is never a bad thing, and I had a lovely time – it was so chilled, and we didn't have to rush anywhere to meet friends, or spend ages in the car going to meet people because Mummy's too much of a try-hard to make them come to us once in a while. It was just delightful. I wish I could spend every day like this.

5th September

Back to the endless activities today, and this one was quite the trip – we went to the theatre. To watch a comedy gig. With the other NCT mummies and Mummy's friend Anna (Lily and Tilda's mummy). This was a mixing of friendship groups, which Mummy is always very nervous about (not quite sure why), which meant I had to mix friendship groups, and all the other NCT babies thought Tilda was my friend. To be fair, she can sit up pretty much now, and was actually quite funny, so I didn't look like quite the loser that I thought I would. Wasn't quite so impressed with amount of attention James the beloved was giving her, but I'm putting this down the fact she had her Freddie the Firefly with her, not her actual charisma and charm. Both of which there is a distinct lack.

6th September

The day started quite well, as I woke early and thought I'd have a little feed, and then snuggle into Mummy for a very rare lie-in. Mummy is not so good at lie-ins nowadays, so she left me surrounded by pillows in what she thought was a safe little haven. Ha! She vastly underestimated my climbing and pillow-scaling abilities.

I waited until she'd just checked up on me, and spotted my opportunity. I'd always wanted to know what happens when you crawl off the side of the bed. Turns out you fall onto the floor.

I bashed my nose and screamed blue murder and sure enough, I got Mummy's attention very quickly and she raced in, screaming, 'Shit, shit, she's fallen off the bed!' as she was on the phone to Grandma. Hardly the calming influence I needed in this situation.

I screamed a bit more, but eventually calmed down, as I spotted the pendant on her necklace and wanted to poke it. God, I love that pendant.

Mummy cleaned up the minute amount of blood, and kept cuddling me loads, and saying sorry. It's lucky I'm not able to be accountable for my actions, as it was definitely my fault, but I'm happy for Mummy to take the blame and let me play with anything I want today to appease her guilt: phones, TV remotes and drawer handles, here I come!

I heard her debate on the phone to her friend whether to tell Daddy or not... she came clean in the end. I think he knew better than to criticise her.

7th September

My cute little nose is ruined! It's covered in a massive brown/red scab that makes me look like a cross between a teddy bear and an out-of-season Rudolph. And annoyingly today, we went to a food festival (my second one in a week, my parents clearly think we're middle class), so I looked ridiculous when I was trying to show off and talk to all the people there.

I went on my first train, which was great, because I got to crawl around on a table for a change, meaning that objects which are usually quite difficult for me to reach were easily accessible. People's glasses, phones, necklaces, bag straps. Perfect!

Mummy carried me in the sling whilst she slugged a prosecco at 10:40am with Nanny. Not the brightest of moves when you have a baby with a massive scab on her nose. God knows what people thought.

She foolishly (maybe she was drunk from the sip she managed to get) held her glass in front of me, and I managed to swipe it a number of times, resulting in a lot of prosecco on the floor. Success!

Whilst there, I had a fascinating discussion with an apiarist. Who knew bees were so amazing? He told me that queen bees carry 60,000 sperm in their bodies, and occasionally get de-throned and murdered by being surrounded and killed by the heat of their worker bees.

Not inappropriate at all for a nearly eight-month-old.

He then asked if I wanted some honey. He clearly hasn't been to a weaning session with the health visitor. Doesn't he know honey is the syrup of the devil for babies under one?

Anyway, all in all a good day. Hoping I'll wake up tomorrow and the scab will have gone, and my nose will be returned to its normal cuteness.

10th September

Mummy and Daddy took me to a very strange place today; a place called a nursery. There were lots of children and babies there, and the women all wore the same coloured tops, and there was an absolute shedload of toys. And also some very poor pieces of artwork that I'm not sure why you would display. The colouring was out of the lines, and sequins were stuck in random places. These people are clearly very careless.

It had a really strange smell as well. A bit like a hospital, but with a definite hint of child rather than old person. I'm not sure I liked it.

Anyway, I was my usual charming self, smiling at everyone as we walked around all the different rooms. The lady kept saying that when I'm there, I'll be doing this and that. I think she must have been mistaken, as these children didn't have their mummies and daddies there (maybe it's like a fun orphanage?) and my parents would never be so cruel as to leave me with people who have no taste in art and a funny odour. I'll spend all my days playing with Mummy forever. I just know it.

Month 9:

A lovely holiday and an assault

13th September

I've been thinking about it, and ever since Cry-gate back in August, I've been giving the parentals an easy ride on the nap-time front. I'm a bit grotty with my cold and today I thought, sod it, I'm going to do what I want. Never mind the fact Daddy has been working nights so we're meant to be VERY quiet all day, or that I kept Mummy up all night, so she only had five hours' broken sleep. This naptime, I was going to do things my way. This was my plan of attack:

Stage 1: When I got put down at my usual time, I just flat refused to go to sleep. I didn't want to waste energy on screaming, so I moaned and bashed my dummies against the cot bars; so much so, I knew Mummy would cave and bring me back downstairs, so I didn't wake Daddy.

Stage 2: I didn't let Mummy put me down anywhere. I start to wobble the old bottom lip, and she's a sucker for it. She even had to have a wee with me on her lap, ha! I got to watch *Peppa Pig* AND suck the remote.

Stage 3: I knew she'd try and put me back down at some point, so I tricked her into thinking I was ready, with the odd eye-rub and slow suck on my dummy, and then *boom*! As soon as she put me down again, I screamed.

To be fair, she was quite resilient. It wasn't until Daddy texted to say I'd woken him up that she started the long climb of defeat up the stairs, to come and get me. My master stroke was making sure I was flat on my tummy as she slowly creaked the door open, so she'd think I might sleep after all, and start to go back downstairs again. Ha! I'll show them I'll nap when I want to.

Stage 4: I'd planned to repeat this over and over until I heard Mummy say 'feck this', and I could avoid the nap a little longer.

I failed at Stage 4, as then it was so bloody comfy lying down that I may have drifted off...

15th September

Went to Sophie's (Lily and Tilda's older sister) sixth birthday party today, and it can probably be described best as absolute bloody carnage. Anna had invited a lot of people and booked some circus entertainers to fit in with the theme (*The Greatest Showman*). It turns out that everybody who had been invited wanted to come, and Anna didn't get the drop-out she had expected.

As we turned up, Anna was literally throwing ham sandwiches at five- and six-year-olds, as they leapt like salmon to catch them in mid-air. It was rather impressive, but I knew despite my generally quite advanced motor skills that I wouldn't have a chance against them, so we stayed a while and then went to Niccy's, where I thought I would get Edie all to myself... hurrah! It would be my chance to show her how much fun I can be now I can crawl and babble. It started well, but then Lauren turned up with Teddy and Bertie, and Edie wanted to play with them. Gutted.

Teddy wanted to give me lots of cuddles and kisses, which I thought was a bit forward, but in spite of the serious encroachment on my personal space, it was really lovely. I think Daddy was keeping his eye on him, and wasn't particularly pleased when Teddy kept coming and shouting, 'Is she asleep yet?' when Daddy was trying to put me down for my nap. Needless to say, I didn't sleep at all.

It was quite the day, as then we went to Great Aunt Jo Jo's house, which I love because there I am the centre of everything. The great cousins still argue over who plays with me, which is cute. Anyway, we watched the football whilst I had my tea, and then I was put to bed for the night, or so they thought.

Last time they tried to get me to stay over there, it was that bad that Cry-gate was put in place, so they should have known it's not an environment conducive to sleep. Ended up keeping Mummy awake for two hours in the middle of the night, as she desperately tried to shove her nipple in my mouth to keep me quiet and not wake everyone else up. She was successful, as she didn't even wake Daddy up, and he was right next to us. She didn't seem quite so pleased with this. I swear she was deliberately knocking into him at one point.

17th September

I am having THE best time ever. I'm on holiday with Mummy and Daddy (I'm always with them, which is not so exciting), but we're also with Grandma and Grandad, which is amazing.

They find absolutely everything I do hilarious and have endless time to play with me, crawl around with me, and read to me. They hang off my every babble. I've also learnt that if I scrunch my nose up when I smile at them, they think I'm even cuter. To be fair, I've heard Mummy say her ovaries contract when I do it, so it must be good, as she's never said that before.

We've been doing all sorts of awesome stuff... swimming, looking for red squirrels (we saw two!), and today we went to what some would describe as a blinged-up farm; others would consider it a really shit zoo. There were the usual animals you hear about from Old MacDonald, but also meerkats and snakes, and hissing cockroaches. There was a butterfly house, which was quite good, especially because my Daddy was definitely scared of them and tried not to show it.

By far, the best bit was the soft play. Grandma took me in there, soon followed by Mummy and Daddy, and I could clamber everywhere and attempt to go down a slide, and just be free.

An old lady was looking at me, so I flashed her a smile.

She kept watching, so I carried on doing it every time I did something clever, like licking a block. You've got to keep your fans happy.

I decided to sleep through last night for the first time in a while, which I thought would make Mummy happy after the weekend. Turns out the fact I fed twice the three nights before meant she didn't sleep so well on her lumpy breasts. There's no pleasing some people.

19th September

My holiday continues to be great, albeit very soggy. Turns out there are limited indoor activities where we are, so we scraped the barrel and went to a sea zoo.

On paper, this made sense, as I do love my Grandad's tropical fish. However, this sea zoo was showcasing British sea life, which are not renowned for their bright and attention-grabbing colours. It turns out 99% of British sea life is grey, brown, or sandy-coloured, and incredibly hard to spot when you're eight months old. The only things I could see were the jellyfish and sea bass, which scared the shit out of me (literally). I did see the red tentacle of an octopus that teased me with the potential of coming out, but it never did, so my excitement was short-lived.

In spite of the sea zoo wash-out, I did get to try a scone today, which is pretty much the first sugary treat I've been allowed. I get the impression that my Mummy continues to make up the rules about weaning to suit her. But right now, I'm on a scone-high, so who cares?

23rd September

Teeth can do one. Who needs them anyway? I've done pretty well so far with only two, and can gum most things into submission, so I feel any more are unnecessary.

Anyway, they're back with a vengeance, and I'm in agony. And I'm letting everyone know about it. Including Mummy's three childless friends that came to stay last night. I mean, I was still delightful, and throwing them the odd cute nose-scrunch smiles that were so successful with Grandma and Grandad, but then I would only settle in Mummy's arms.

This meant that when they came back from the pub, they had to entertain themselves, and eventually just went to bed, when they'd been expecting a bit of a late one, as Mummy was busy with me. What made it slightly funny is that Mummy had a night out with her school friends the night before last, and didn't get to bed till 4:30am, so was already mega-tired and trying her best to hide it.

In the end, I got to sleep with Mummy and Daddy, and they were that desperate they'd maxed out my Nurofen quota by 3am.

Mummy got all panicked in the morning, when I was still moaning, so ended up taking me to the out-of-hours doctor and leaving her friends to make breakfast and lock up the house. She's hardly the hostess with the mostess.

I feel really sorry for doctors, because all they see is poorly, sad people, so I decided that I'd chirp up a bit. Upon crossing the doctor's threshold, I threw her some cheeky smiles, tried to steal the stethoscope from her, and generally seemed like I was absolutely fine. I liked her. Apart from when she shoved that wooden stick in my mouth. Not OK.

She diagnosed teething. Shocker.

25th September

Argh, my mouth is on fire! I've got four bloody teeth coming at the same time. I've been suffering beyond compare for the last couple of days, and today has been the worst. I can tell Mummy and Daddy have been getting frustrated with me. I don't think they've cottoned on about the teeth, despite the doctor's diagnosis.

I couldn't have been any more obvious over the last few days: hand-gnawing; constant drooling; bipolar attitude during the day; nightmare at night. It still took a lovely friend of Mummy's at Rhythm Time yesterday to make her realise I've pushed one of them through already! Which I think I should get more recognition for.

It wasn't until I lost my shit on the way back from Baby Sensory; and Mummy had to pull over into a layby (one of my old favourites, as it happens) that she realised the other three were searing their way through. Then she felt mega sorry for me. So much so, she wasn't even that angry when I dropped two dummies and my favourite *Finding Nemo* ball in the only stream of urine in the whole layby. She thinks it was a fluke, and clearly doesn't see my potential as a future Goal Attack.

I could see her, albeit momentarily, consider whether she could just sterilise the dummies, given they are such a precious commodity. Luckily, she realised it was not appropriate, seeing as they were covered in gravel and stranger-piss.

When I got home, I cried for Daddy, but then when I got to him, I remembered how lovely Mummy has been, up in the middle of the night with me, so cried to go back to her. But then Daddy is tall and gives me a greater view, so I cried to go back to him. But Mummy looked tired, so... you get the picture.

Then, wonder of wonders, they rubbed this A-mazing liquid on my gums. Where has this been? Why didn't my parents find this before, with their incessant Googling, the last time I got teeth? It says you can only put it on every three hours. I'm going to ensure I make enough noise to get it at least every thirty minutes.

Anyway, this wonder-cure worked so well that I even permitted a sneaky pub trip. Managed to get five reads of *Bobby the Bunny* whilst there so Daddy could finish his pint. Result.

28th September

I've had a right time of it over the last couple of days. Friday got off to a reasonable start. Daddy left at 5:45am to go and watch the Ryder Cup at the golf club, so it was a Mummy-and-me day, and I thought I'd give her an easy ride, with only a minor kick-off about being put down for my morning nap.

I then, being ever the philanthropist, went to a Macmillan coffee morning, where I successfully managed to lick a bench when Mummy was eating a scone and trying to drink her tea. Not quite as yummy as the scone, but I liked the feel of it on my tongue. I also kicked off a little bit, as I couldn't join in with the older boys and girls running around, and instead they tried to force me to play with Tilda. She can't even point her finger yet, so not quite sure what we're meant to play when pointing at random objects is out of the window.

Typically, Mummy packed too much into our day, so we had to rush over to meet my beloved James. We had a great time fighting over a little coolbag, and screeching at each other across the table whilst they attempted a civilised wine and lunch. Sometimes I think they only get the sandwich to make the wine more acceptable.

As it got closer to teatime, my teeth really started to play up, so I was justifiably grumpy. I was just settling down to eat more cucumber when I started to feel a bit funny, and had an urge to cuddle Mummy. I never do this, but it felt really lovely. I felt funnier and funnier, and went into a sort of trance, and the next thing I knew, I was lying in Mummy's arms, all pale and grey and limp. For some reason, this really freaked her out, and I got bundled into the car very quickly and Daddy was driving very fast (good job he's a policeman).

I felt much better after about twenty minutes, and by the time Mummy and Daddy were talking to the lovely lady behind the counter at A&E and telling her about this episode, I was back to full fitness. I even managed to throw her a few smiles, to make her broody and show her I was fine.

Then a man in a blue tunic came to see me, and I threw him a few smiles and pointed at him until he touched my finger. They kept attaching this really annoying thing to my toe, so I wriggled non-stop for ages, to try and get it off. I found that if I stayed still long enough for them to say, 'Just a few more seconds and we'll have a trace,' and then moved, I got the most attention from everyone.

After ages being sat in this room with lots of other people who were not quite as jolly as me, some of whom smelt quite a bit as well, we went through to "Majors", which sounded very grand. I found loads of things funny in this place (apart from the needle they shot into my foot), so was laughing away as lots of machines were buzzing and making funny noises whilst people were groaning.

I heard Mummy tell numerous people, 'I've not got

Munchausen's-by-proxy, I promise! She was really limp and grey.' They gave my mummy a knowing look, said it happens all the time, and showed me to Dr Ben. He was lovely and knew to touch my finger when I pointed it at him, and tickled my feet, and generally looked quite bemused by me. Then we went home as it turns out there was nothing they could find that was wrong with me.

29th September

Not so great a day, as I've vommed a lot. Mostly in Mummy and Daddy's bed (which Mummy insisted I slept in after last night's episode). I'm not that bothered by the sick. It doesn't taste great, but as soon as I've lurched up to sitting and expelled my torrent of vomit, I'm happy as Larry, and try and drift off again, but apparently I'm not allowed to sleep in it, so I kept getting woken up and changed and baby-wiped, whilst they changed the sheets. They need to chill out, it's only a bit of vom.

Managed to scare the parentals further this evening, as I developed a solitary red mark on my back. Not a spot or rash, just a mark. But you can imagine the panic this induced in everyone. After a photoshoot of my mark and a call to Grandma and Grandad, I was deemed OK to go to sleep. Thank God. I am knackered.

30th September

I've had my first bath with Mummy. I don't think it was quite the peaceful, serene, bonding experience she had envisioned, given it was 1:30 in the morning, and we were both covered in vomit, but I had a whale of a time. Why they wouldn't let me play with my bath toys, I don't know. But Mummy's saggy breasts were quite the funbags, and were sufficient entertainment.

The absolute bonus was that I managed to wee and poo over Daddy, who then needed a shower. I heard him mutter, 'We're never having another one,' numerous times, which Mummy did not seem to find helpful at all.

Then I moaned a little, stroked Mummy's face a little (which made her well up a bit, the weirdo), and then snuggled in for more sleep.

5ᵗʰ October

I think my mummy might have been abducted, as she left this morning and still wasn't back by bath and bedtime. She's never left me for this long before. Although I'm not sure how many abductees carry a suitcase, and skip off up the driveway with a carefree attitude, towards their friend's car?!

I'm a bit worried about her, but not that worried that I couldn't enjoy my lovely day with Nanny, Daddy and Uncle Rhys. Nanny bought me some new books (I personally didn't think I needed more than *Dear Zoo* and *Bobby the Bunny*, as they're just the best). They're awesome, though, and I managed to get everyone to read them to me fifty-six times. Each.

We also had a delightful lunch at M&S café. My nanny loves M&S. They just offer that extra bit of quality, apparently.

Hope Mummy comes back tomorrow. I miss her, and her smell, and her goofy smile. Not as much as I miss her milk, though. They keep trying to offer me some other kind of milk in a bottle. Apparently, I've had it before. I'm not falling for that, though. They must think I'm stupid.

6th October

Mummy is back! Well, at least, I think she is. A woman who smells a bit like Mummy, sounds a bit like Mummy, and wears her pendant necklace, is in my house. But she is wearing a mask. And has that stench of vomit that I remember from last week.

Daddy had to go and pick her up from her "spa break" as they are referring to it (apparently, she deserved some "me time"?) early, because she woke up and was sick everywhere. A just reward for her wanting to spend thirty-six hours away from me.

Now she's quarantined away from me, upstairs. I'm only allowed to see her when I need milk, and then I get whisked away again. I'm quite glad, as that mask is freaky, and makes her sound like Darth Vader.

8th October

Mummy left me again today, this time to go to "work". She looked very smart. Although she had to leave work early, as Daddy rang saying he'd been to the loo five times in two hours and was nervous he'd caught the bug from the weekend. Turns out he'd just eaten too much fruit the day before. By the time Mummy rushed home, he was eating crisps on the sofa whilst I napped.

The enormous and exaggerated eye-roll Mummy gave behind Daddy's back indicated she was less than happy at Daddy's untimely bowel movements.

I'm beginning to get a bit worried about how much she is leaving me, so I make sure that when she comes back I never leave her side. And I get her to pick me up all the time. And if she puts me down, I cry most of the time. Not all the time, though. Nobody likes a moaner.

9th October

Oh my God, I have been the victim of a traumatic assault! And it was completely unprovoked! I was just minding my own business, playing with a large, foam letter E when this big boy (he was at least quadruple my age) stole it from me.

So I touched his plastic truck just to see what it was like, and he whacked me over the head with it! Needless to say, I was very upset, and screamed a lot. Mummy was crying, I was crying. It was very sad. I did the whole mouth-wide-open-but-no-sound-coming-out kind of cry, to show just how upset I was, and kept looking over at the boy, hoping to see some remorse.

He showed none!

And he didn't get told off, because Mummy wasn't aware of the social etiquette in such incidents, and didn't know what to do because his mummy wasn't watching.

It was all very traumatic, apart from when Mummy tried to put an ice pack on my head. That was just funny, so I kept batting it away and laughing.

10th October

I have played THE best tricks on Mummy today. It's Baby Sensory Wednesday, so Mummy packed me up into the car for my nap and headed off. I did the classic "straining" noises around six minutes into the drive, so Mummy detoured for our usual Morrisons pre-Baby Sensory nappy change. With a "fuck my life" attitude, Mummy carted me into the baby change, unpacked all the changing equipment from the bag, laid me down, and unpopped me to assess the damage.

And she found... nothing. I'd barely had time to wee! Haha! I'd conned her with the noises, and she hadn't waited for the confirmatory stench. What a fool! She was that perplexed by the lack of faeces she even forgot to do her normal fake browse of the magazine section.

The day got even better when, at Baby Sensory, I managed to wee on her. It was water messy play week (I would hardly call a few rubber ducks and sponges in 1mm of water a sensory experience, but heyho), and about seven of us were crammed in our nappies in this paddling pool. Another baby joined us, and burst into tears, which set the next baby off. It made me consider my internal happiness about being semi-naked in lukewarm water surrounded by other semi-naked babies, some of whom I haven't met before, and subsequently I started crying.

After the adults had nervously laughed at how funny it

was (which it wasn't), Mummy pulled me out and bundled me up in a towel. As she did so, she dislodged my nappy just enough to expose me. I bided my time and, just when she thought we were having a really lovely bonding moment popping bubbles together, I looked lovingly into her eyes and weed. All over her crotch. Ha! Even better, she had to wear the jeans all day.

11th October

Met with my beloved James today. I have to admit, he did look rather dashing in some tweed dungarees. I wish Mummy had put a bit more thought into my outfit, although I think he's pretty smitten already. He was certainly watching in awe as I plundered his packet of raisins with lightning speed.

We went to soft play. The best bit was that I got to lick about seven massive green balls. I even managed to lick one whilst going down a slide on Mummy's knee. I am living the dream.

There were animals at this place, too. I got so tantalisingly close to shoving my finger up a calf's nostril because Mummy was distracted talking to her friend, but she caught me just in time. Gutted.

Month 10: Nursery

12th October

I am the big nine months today, so cue the usual fiasco of me posing with the "hilarious" update Mummy has written. Made sure I moved really quickly for the whole time, so any photo was really blurry.

Went to Anna's house. Found a tiny little googly eye on the carpet, and managed to sneak it into my mouth and store it in my cheek. Unfortunately, Mummy spotted it before I could swallow it, which was thoroughly disappointing. I quite liked the idea of my poo having a little eye staring from it to freak Mummy out.

13th October

Enjoying reading a new novel at the moment: *Rabbit's Nap*. I love lifting the flaps. I've nailed the "pull down" and the "pull to the side" ones, but the bastard Builder Bear one lifts upwards, and I can't figure out how to bloody do it. Damn my lack of fine motor skills. My favourite is the mouse band, because my mummy says 'Squeak, squeak' at this bit, and it's just totally hilarious. Every time.

The one thing I don't get is the tortoise on a bike. Surely his legs would move too slowly to maintain momentum, and he would just fall off? But perhaps I'm over-thinking it.

We went to see some of Mummy's friends for tea and cake, although I wasn't actually allowed any cake. I had carrots and hummus instead. Double standards.

My mummy and her friends put me in a wig. I looked hilarious, apparently. One for my 18th, and all that.

Can't wait.

15th October

Another day, another sabotage of Mummy's utopian idea of maternity leave. She thought she could have a lovely, long last play visit with James and his mummy before she goes back to work next week. They chose a venue that served alcohol at 10am, yet claimed to be a soft play for children. Needless to say, they needed minimal encouragement to have a sneaky prosecco just after midday, with their lunch.

Mummy ordered a snack plate for me, despite having brought a full packed lunch with us, as she got scared when the sign said only food and drink bought on the premises were to be consumed, and she hates to be a rule-breaker. I contemplated a slice of cucumber, but it was chopped differently to the way Mummy does it, so I just left it. I wasn't really feeling hungry.

Had a bit of a play, licked a few soft play items, but then started to feel really ill, so Mummy had to take me home as I was boiling hot. 39.6 degrees Celsius of boiling hot.

You can imagine the panic this induced in Mummy. She even stopped halfway home, to check I was still breathing. She hasn't done that since the early days.

I've recently decided I don't like Calpol. It's gross, and nowhere near as nice as Nurofen, so I clamped my jaws together when Mummy attempted to give it to me. I

194

made her wait till I was crying, then she tried to force-feed it to me. I choked and vommed it back up anyway.

I still felt really poorly; so much so that I started shaking with a fever, so after a late-night FaceTime with Grandma and Grandad (where Mummy cried... again!), I was whisked off to their house for a sleepover. Although I didn't really sleep. And I had maxed out my Nurofen dosage by 3am.

16th October

I feel so poorly. I'm pretty sure no baby has ever felt as poorly as I do right now.

Apart from the occasional fifteen minutes post-Calpol-induced bout of energy, where I crawl around a bit, I just want to cuddle my mummy (and only my mummy) and watch *In the Night Garden*, which I saw for the first time today.

I don't know if it's the fact I'm dosed up to the max on strawberry-flavoured drugs, but this TV programme is seriously weird. Why does Makka Pakka clean and sleep with stones? Why is Iggle Piggle the only one that can leave the Night Garden? Why is Upsy Daisy constantly lifting her skirt, and the Tombliboos always dropping their trousers? Why don't the Pontipines and Wottingers just leave notes, or call each other, rather than continuously chasing each other around? And what the feck are the Tittifers and Haahoos?

I'm too tired to find the answers after watching eight episodes of it with Mummy. She seems equally perplexed by it. Grandma hasn't got a clue, and keeps getting all their names wrong.

17th October

It turns out I have hand, foot and mouth disease. Although my spots are on my arms, legs and around my bumhole (Mummy laughs every time she says "bumhole". I have no idea why), which just makes no sense. But I'm contagious, so can't see anyone, which is annoying, as I feel perfectly fine and have been tearing around the house all day.

Because I've been house-bound, I've managed to practise pulling myself up on most items around the house now, and can open the kitchen cupboards and pull stuff out. It's just the best fun.

I've also started to scream when I'm in my highchair. I just feel so restrained by it, and much prefer to be fed on Mummy or Daddy's knee, where I can freely slap their jeans and faces with my messy hands, and share my food with them. I really am so kind.

18th October

Mummy left me again today, to go to work. She seemed very pleased to be going. She was away all afternoon and evening, so I refused every bottle I was offered, as I knew Daddy would text her and then she would remember me at home. Without her. Because she's left me. Again.

Carrying on with the whole hating-the-highchair game. I really like seeing them try and dodge my mucky hands, whilst also trying to make it look like not a big deal, as they think that will make me do it more. They're right. It does!

20th October

Another visit with Nanny, another amazing trip to an M&S café. Firstly, I get fussed over by the hordes of old people, and told how cute and smiley I am (which is true, I am), then I get sneaked bits of scones, which I wolf down with surprising rapidity, and finally I get snuggled by my Nanny, which I just love. She had my favourite butterfly necklace on, so I tugged on that for a fair while, which is always good fun.

Then we got to go around the shops, and I pointed towards the Christmas stuff. There was a very cute Christmas dress there, so obviously Nanny bought it for me. I actually meant to point at the reindeer teddy just above it, but my finger didn't quite go where I planned. Ah well, there's always next time.

When we got home, I had the best bath of my life. It was possibly the best time of my life; even better than when Mummy and I jump on the bed like monkeys. I was playing peepo over the side of the bath with Mummy, and it was so funny. Her little face was so cute when she watched me pop up and surprise her. Man, she is easily pleased.

21st October

My Uncle Matt is hilarious. He rang Mummy up, and said he wanted to practise carrying me in the sling for when baby Juan arrives, so we went over to their house and went on a lovely walk. "Juan" is what mummy has decided to nickname her new niece or nephew, and she keeps weirdly giggling to herself about it. I didn't have the heart to tell Matt I've grown considerably since birth, and really can control my own head these days, which Juan won't be able to do for ages, but heyho. It was fun.

Auntie Justine is getting really fat now. And yet people continue to seem very happy with her weight gain. I don't want to make a big deal of it, so just stare at her swollen tummy instead.

We went to the park; we went to Costa; we played on a new rocking dinosaur they had bought. It was just amazing. I made Uncle Matt follow me round the house, crawling for ages. Whenever he looked tired, I shot him my cutest little smile and giggled at him, and he'd be hooked in for another ten minutes. Sucker.

Looking at Juan's room, it has more toys and clothes than I do. Something tells me Uncle Matt and Auntie Justine are somewhat more prepared than my mummy and daddy were for me. Plus, apparently Uncle Matt has just discovered Facebook Marketplace, which may have a lot to answer for.

Then we went for a meal for Grandad's birthday. I was having a fab time playing with Grandma, who is just the best at making up silly games, but then it started to get a bit late. They tried to palm me off with weird crisps that melted in my mouth and tasted funny (but were surprisingly moreish), until I just lost it and we had to leave halfway through the main course. Mummy and Daddy thought I'd fall asleep in the car on the way home. Ha! Instead, I made Mummy sing six renditions of *Say Hello to the Sun* till we got home. Her voice may be terrible, but it's my terrible.

22nd October

I am officially a pet-owner. My grandad bought me some fish today, to stay at his house. The two best ones are called Emily and James (obviously), and are a pair of little lovefish. They follow each other around the tank, just like James tries to follow me when we're together (although I'm way too quick for him).

The best thing was that when we went to pick them, there were so many fish, it was amazing. I banged on all the tanks, and I almost managed to grab some pondweed for a tasty snack, but disappointingly Mummy spotted it before I could take a bite.

Then we went to see Great Grandma and Great Grandad. Today, he called me Gertrude. This is the least favourite name he has called me so far. I still can't tell whether he is joking, or if he genuinely doesn't know who I am. Great Grandma regaled us with the old 'Last time you came, do you remember when the two girls didn't know what to make of each other?'

Yes, I remember the Beast. How could I forget? Yes, it was awkward. She was a lot bigger than me, and I got scared. And it wasn't the last time. I've visited seven times since.

24th October

Baby Sensory graduation. What a ridiculous concept. You basically get a certificate for your Mummy paying £5 a session and driving you there. I didn't have to actually do anything. Then you have to wear a ridiculous cap and gown, which are itchy and make you cry, all while your mummy is dangling a rattle in your face to try and get a cute photo. I'm not going back there again. Which is kind of a given, seeing as I've graduated.

25th October

My mummy is an embarrassment on many levels.

Firstly, she buys me ridiculous fancy dress outfits that she thinks I'll look cute in. Yes, I probably will look cute, because I'm a baby dressed as a pumpkin, or a Christmas pudding, but that's not the point.

Secondly, she just does embarrassing things. All the time. She banged her heel on the shopping trolley, because I made her carry me and pull the heavy trolley along as I obviously refused to sit in it. I find if you lift your legs and make them super straight (as though you're already sitting) the moment they try to move you towards the trolley, it is nigh on impossible for anyone to get you in there. Genius. Anyway, her foot started bleeding, so she shoved a wet wipe (the only mildly absorbent material she could find in the baby bag, aside from a nappy) down the back of her shoe. She then continued to shop with a bloody wet wipe flapping out the back of her shoe as she hobbled about, and three different people came and told her she'd got something stuck to her shoe. She went bright red as she explained what had happened, and tried to blame me. What an idiot.

27th October

Apparently, we're in the middle of a fun-filled family weekend away. However, there have definitely been some bits that have not been such fun. Like the journey down here last night. Mummy thought that if we set off at bedtime, I'd sleep all the way and transition into the travel cot without even a stir. Because that kind of plan always works, doesn't it? Fool.

I woke after two hours of the journey and started to scream as, quite frankly, I didn't know where the feck I was. Mummy had to scramble through to the back of the car whilst on the motorway (hilarious to watch) and sing the Baby Sensory song to keep me quiet. I would just about drift off and then she'd stop so I'd wake again. It took them a good thirty minutes before they realised that they could just play the song on YouTube.

In total, we listened to it twenty-four-and-a-half times non-stop before we arrived at their friends' house. Even I was a little bored by the end.

Anyway, obviously I refused to go to sleep in the travel cot for another hour or so, because I liked the thought of Mummy and Daddy trying to act all cool in front of their friends whilst I was babbling at the monitor and trying to escape my netted prison.

In the end, I dropped off, which was disappointing, but I redeemed myself about two hours later by waking and screaming again. Cue another night in Mummy and Daddy's bed whilst Mummy tried to quieten me with her nipple or the dummy, and Daddy pretended to be/was actually asleep.

Today has been much better. I've made a new friend called Seren, who is really grown-up. Almost as grown up as Edie. She can walk and say, 'Oh dear,' and eat a yoghurt by herself. And she can refuse a nap all day. Ledge.

We went to a farm, where Mummy had to pretend she was OK feeding some savage-looking goats from her hand. Mummy tried to give me this awful pasta dish that Seren's mummy had cooked. Bleurgh. I just kept batting it away and clamping my mouth shut to make sure everyone, including the chef, could see what I thought of this culinary disaster. Mummy seemed quite embarrassed by this, but it was nothing compared to how red she went when I also refused the tea-time offering of homemade cottage pie. Gross!

28th October

I LOVE SOFT PLAY! That is all.

30th October

I've been conned – by my own mother, no less! Yesterday, Mummy took me to this new place (although it did smell vaguely familiar, and I swear I've seen the poor-quality artwork somewhere before), and I got to play with lots of toys. She was busy chatting to this lady all about me, and how I nap, and won't take the bottle, blah, blah, blah. Every so often, I turned round, and she wasn't there, but that was fine, as she was probably just making a cup of tea, or going for a wee. Or so I thought...

There was a lovely girl called Ottilie, and a cheeky boy called Lucas, who kept giving me a ball but then pulling it back and laughing just before I could grab it. He thought it was hilarious. I thought he was a bit of an annoying tool.

After I'd explored every toy in the room, Mummy was back, and we went home, and I thought no more about it. I loved it, despite the funny smell. Mummy kept looking sad whenever she smelt me at home afterwards, which was weird. In fact, she looked pretty sad full stop.

Anyway, today we went back. Only this time, Mummy left me. For a whole 165 minutes! It was awful. I thought she'd gone for good, and I didn't know anyone except Ottilie and, to be fair, although she's clearly older than me, she can't tell me much apart from 'Hiya' and 'dog'.

Every time the door opened, I thought it was Mummy, so I rushed over, and it wouldn't be her, and it was just so horrible. I cried. A lot. I decided the only thing for it was to make sure Shannon, my keyworker (whatever that means), was always near me, as she seemed like a responsible adult. To ensure she couldn't leave my side for the whole 165 minutes, I cried whenever she stood up. This meant she had to crawl around all the time next to me, which was quite fun, actually.

Obviously, I shunned the milk she offered me from the bottle. And from the doidy cup. And the sippy cup. I mean, do they seriously think I'd fall for that? And there was no way I was taking a nap and closing my eyes when annoying Lucas was about.

Eventually, after I'd made Shannon stay with me the whole time, and sabotaged whatever Ottilie was playing with (she was not so keen on this), and shown off my acrobatics when my nappy was changed, Mummy came back. I was so happy to see her face. Although she weirdly was crying when she picked me up and cuddled me. But I didn't care. I'm never going to be mean to her again, as long as she never leaves me there again. I'm sure she won't. I made it clear I didn't like it.

31st October

My first Halloween, and I'm ill. Mummy had to cancel the NCT party she had arranged at our house. I'm actually not that poorly, I was just in a bad mood this morning and got one spot near (not even on) my hand, which Mummy was then convinced was hand, foot and mouth again. I'm regretting being grumpy, as I've only really got a runny nose, and it means I won't get to battle with the other babies over my toys, or see my beloved James.

I bet he looked so handsome in his astronaut suit (I'd argue not that scary, but apparently his auntie bought it for him, and his mummy didn't want to fork out for another outfit, even if it was two sizes too small... I can see why she and my mummy get on so well). The only good thing is, I was relieved from having to be dressed up as a bloody pumpkin by Mummy. What a cliché. She has no imagination.

The last couple of days, I've decided I'm an independent woman, and am way too mature to need someone else to feed me. I'm nearly ten months, so I most definitely have the motor skills to feed myself. But only at lunchtimes. If anyone even tries to put a spoon near my mouth at a lunchtime, I scream and knock it away (unless it's a fruit pot; they're the exception because they're so bloody scrumptious), and I will only eat things I can put into my mouth myself. And only if they are covered in hummus or Dairylea. At teatime, I'm absolutely fine with Mummy feeding me from the spoon, because... well, just because. And I only need half the things to be covered in Dairylea or hummus at teatime.

2nd November

I spoke too soon. I was dressed as a pumpkin today. How unoriginal. I was all for cutting up my blue Ryder Cup baby vest, covering it in blood and going as Brexit, but Mummy thought it would be too political.

We went to a Halloween party at Anna's house, and it was the scariest thing ever. When I walked in, there was child-sized alien king just stood there, waving a sword at me. Obviously, I burst into tears, and we had to leave the party for ten minutes before we could try again.

Once I got into the swing of it, though, it was OK. Mummy kept trying to make me play with Tilda, but the ten weeks between us is still very telling, and she just can't keep up with me. She can't even clap yet. So instead, I tried to play with Edie, but she kept shunning me. When it is just the two of us, she loves playing with me, and we give each other things, and she gives me vice-like hugs and pretends to change my nappy.

But today I kept trying to give her things and follow her around, and pull at her vampire cloak, but she just ignored me. She wanted to play with Lily; just because she's two-and-a-half, and obviously cooler. I was that perplexed, I ate a meal without any hummus or Dairylea.

The "danger" drive home at 6:30 was fun, though, as Mummy was very, very happy after drinking a number of glasses of prosecco, so whilst Daddy navigated us home,

Mummy sang me lots of songs where she made up the lyrics in a bid to keep me awake. She is hilarious.

3rd November

I have had the BEST day. I have been to somewhere called Blackpool. It had everything: lights; the sea; fish and chips; arcades; more lights; a huge, tall tower; lots of lovely seagulls, and a lot of tourists (some of whom look like there is something small yet significant missing from their genetic make-up). I think I might live there when I grow up.

We went with Uncle Matt, the ever-growing Auntie Justine, and Mummy. Mummy said Daddy was playing golf again. Again.

I made sure I continued my quest to show my auntie and uncle what life is going to be like for them soon, by being so utterly cute and smiley, and then occasionally losing it (just to keep them on their toes). Lunchtime was the best, as Mummy made Uncle Matt clear up the aftermath. I've got really good at launching food at angles, so it scatters everywhere. I think he really enjoyed that part, in particular. Juan is onto a winner with him, because as soon as I started to cry, he whacked out his phone and put *Teletubbies* on, which is my second-favourite show. Result. Po and Lala are definitely my favourites. Tinky Winky gives me the creeps.

The day was made even better by the fact my mummy revealed a previously hidden super-power. She is amazing at the donkey derby. She's a bloody machine! So much so, she beat a full field of players and won me the

BIGGEST teddy ever. He is so snuggly. I keep biting him to show him I love him. I do get left with a mouthful of fur when I do this, but I think that just shows what a high-quality toy he is.

Managed to get Dairylea for lunch and tea. Could there be a better day?

5th November

So, despite making it very clear I did not enjoy my time in nursery, Mummy left me there again today. For a whole six hours. That's ages.

I want to be really angry about it, as Mummy should never leave me. Ever. But I actually had a great time. There was a ball pit; we sang songs with people that had lovely and tuneful voices; I even did some painting. I don't get this kind of service at home. I refused all food (except a biscuit, for obvious reasons), sleep and milk, as I don't want Mummy to feel in any way comfortable with leaving me there. But it was great. I even lay still for nappy changes as I was so chilled out.

Ottilie was there. I think she can definitely teach me some helpful tricks of the trade. Lucas was also there, and did the annoying ball non-sharing game again. It's really not funny. Especially as I fall for it every time and hold my hand out. Must make a mental note not to do that.

Grandma and Auntie Justine came to pick me up with Mummy. I couldn't see Grandma at first, so I rushed over to Mummy but then I pushed Mummy away and cuddled Grandma as she's my fave. Mummy looked like she might cry again. Well, it's her own fault for leaving me there.

7th November

Usual start to the day, reading a book in bed with Mummy. Pointed at the ducks in the book when Mummy said 'Quack, quack,' to ensure she continues to consider me a genius, and then we went down to the lounge. And there, in all its glory, was an activity table. Just like the ones from Baby Sensory and nursery.

It's amazing. It literally has everything I could ever wish for. My favourite bit is the phone, which I pick up and hand to Mummy for her to answer, about twenty-five times in a row. She tries to mix it up, by pretending it's various different people on the phone, but I know there's no one there. Why would my Uncle Rhys ring up to ask if I was being a good girl and ate all my lunch? He's got more important things to be getting on with. I think it's more to keep herself amused.

The best thing is, you can press loads of buttons at once, so you can't figure out what does what. It's just a joyous cacophony.

Mummy had to drag me away from the wonder-table, as we went to meet one of her friends who has a baby called Hamish. Now that is a cool name. And he did a cool thing. He managed to vomit in a ball pit at a soft play. That really is living your best life.

Mummy was left in charge of the two of us whilst Hamish's mummy nipped to the loo, and he chose then to do it. Well-played, Hamish. The look of panic on Mummy's face was hilarious. She had to pull out Hamish (who was still erupting like a vomit volcano), whilst also trying to stop me from licking the sick-covered balls. In the end, she just dithered between the two of us, so Hamish managed to get completely soaked in vomit and then crawl in it, and I licked about four balls without her noticing. Yes!

Still managing to keep up the no-spoon-at-lunch rule, so Mummy has to pack a variety of finger foods for wherever we go. I don't know why she bothers. All I'll eat is one stick of cucumber and then crackers covered in hummus or Dairylea. Or both.

9th November

Woke up and had a lovely breakfast, complete with numerous porridge-sneezes. A porridge-sneeze, I've concluded, is the one of the best of all food-sneezes in terms of splatter-distance and parental coverage, second only to a crumpet-sneeze, which are by far the messiest. I think it must be something to do with the stringy yet light texture. Scrambled egg-sneezes sneak in at third.

After the considerable clean-up operation, we went to Edie's party today and I was the first one there, and it meant Edie actually wanted to play with me... until Lily and her friend Molly turned up, and then she ignored me, and just wanted to fight over the Stickman toy with them. I don't really get it as it's just a soft toy stick with a man's face on it but hey, each to their own.

I was left playing with Tilda... again... although, to be fair, she can sit up now, and hold toys, which means I can steal them off her, so that's quite a lot of fun.

I also got to eat some birthday cake, which Mummy got pressured into giving me because everyone else got to have some. I love the look of pure panic on her face as she doesn't want to appear over-bearing and like a member of the anti-sugar Gestapo, whilst also hearing "she'll become addicted to sugar and morbidly obese by one if you give it to her" on loop in her head. Silly Mummy.

After the party, we went to Nanny's house, which involved quite a long car ride. Mummy, in her infinite wisdom, tried to coordinate it with my nap time. HA! I stayed awake the whole time. Mummy has been thinking she's so clever recently, by having a stash of toys and dummies on the front seat that she can reach back and pass to me throughout the journey. Today I developed a strategy to oppose this.

If I throw the toy/dummy to my left, Mummy can reach round and get it if she times it correctly at traffic lights with a swift handbrake-on, seatbelt-off, car-seat-moved-back manoeuvre, so I now make sure I throw it to the right. This way, she can't get it and so, after I've managed to throw all the toys and dummies she has brought, she has to find a layby and pull over so that she can collect them, and we can start the game again. What is even better is that sometimes the toys/dummies fall into dirt or dust (her car is a state) so each time there are fewer toys/dummies she can offer, so we end up stopping loads. Genius!

After the fun-filled trip to Nanny's, I got given possibly the best gift ever. It's noisy, requires endless parental intervention, and is dangerous, as I can easily fall off. It's a ride-on princess car. It has a horn. It has a gearstick that plays different songs. It lights up. Basically, I spent the remainder of the day demanding to be pushed up and down Nanny's lounge on it. Uncle Rhys must love me a lot, as he put in a fair old shift.

10th November

Today I have seen both the most magical and the most scary things ever.

Most scary is Daddy's friend Pete. He is big and bearded and grumpy. I screamed in his face, for obvious reasons.

Most magical – singing reindeers. I don't know what a reindeer is but boy, can they sing. I was entranced. And it's strange, as they're really clever, and only sing when you press a button. Must give them some evolutionary advantage or something.

After the mixed bag of experiences, I got back to Nanny's, and had another first. My first word. I can't understand why Mummy hasn't realised sooner that when I say "A-ka" I clearly mean "cracker". I even point at them, which should have given her a bit of a clue. For the rest of day, Mummy just kept giving me pride-filled gazes, which was rather nice, so I thanked her with a bite on the nipple!

Month 11:

Mummy goes back to work

12th November

Back at bloody nursery again, so I refused my bloody milk again. I'm not sure why they haven't cottoned on that I'm never going to drink it. Lucas was there, being a tool again. Man, that boy is annoying. He keeps doing that stupid ball trick, but has extended it to all objects. I'm getting better at remembering that he's a trickster, but he still gets me with every new object he tries. Argh!

It's also another milestone month-day, so Mummy tried a variety of ways to get me to pose with the piece of paper. Daddy rolled his eyes throughout and Mummy accused him of not caring about the cherished records she's creating. They're written on crappy A4 paper in a Crayola felt tip – she needs to get a grip. In the end, they had to Sellotape the paper to the door and sit me on a swivel chair and time it so I was looking the other way, thus removing the opportunity for me to sabotage it.

The lengths some people will go to just for some likes on Facebook!

15th November

When I heard Mummy and Daddy say we were having a family day, I had my reservations, as it normally ends up with Mummy and Daddy arguing over who should have packed the wipes and who battled with the last poo. I try to be fair and do at least six so they can each have a share, but they still bicker.

However, in spite of my doubts, it was amazing! I went on something called a swing... Holy shit, they're fricking awesome. You basically sit in this uber-comfy seat (most things are comfy when you have a nappy on, to be fair) and swing to and fro, and the more you enjoy it, the more your mummy and daddy push you, and it's just the best. I think I've found my future career... full-time swinger. I've decided if we go anywhere now and there's not a swing, I'm going to lose my shit.

16th November

Ever the drama-queen, Mummy hosted an "end of maternity" party today. I'm not quite sure what one is, given a number of odd things happened:

- Mummy kept crying. In the morning; when friends arrived; when she put me down for my nap; when she got me up from my nap; when I had lunch... you get the picture.

- All her friends kept saying, 'Oh don't worry, you'll get used to it,' and, 'It's just a new way of life, you'll adjust.' Mummy kept agreeing and looking at me with those sad eyes.

- She then kept saying, 'I'm looking forward to having hot cups of tea.' Weird, as I didn't even know tea could be hot. Surely that's dangerous?

- There was prosecco. I thought this was meant for celebrations... although, actually, my mummy will drink it pretty much whenever.

- My mummy cooked! For other people! This never happens.

All in all, a very strange day. It's not like she's leaving me and we're not going to spend all day, every day, together.

Needless to say, I clung to her like a limpet, and refused to go to anyone else. Or smile. All day.

18th November

We went to Chester Zoo today. I think I may have given Mummy and Daddy the impression I like zoos, and I can kind of see why. I love my *Dear Zoo* book, so much so I've ripped half of the flaps, and I can perform a rather exceptional lion roar.

But morally, I disagree with keeping animals caged up. I can completely sympathise with them, as I do hate my jovial prison, and being hemmed in by the constraints of the buggy and the car seat (not to mention modern society). Granted, they potentially have it worse than me, in that the majority of their homes are being destroyed, but do they have to go to nursery? No. So I think it's even.

Anyway, it was wet and cold, most of the animals were sensibly hiding away, and I refused to nap all day, or eat any lunch, so you can imagine how frosty the atmosphere was on the way home. Well, it was until I fell asleep at 4pm, despite Mummy and Daddy, by this point, trying to keep me awake. Mixed messages?!

20th November

I am FUMING! Mummy told me off this morning for biting her nipple. Well, she can feck off if she thinks she's having the joy of me feeding from her again. I don't care if it's only her second day back at work, and she's crying because she thinks it is all her fault, it bloody well is. No one shouts at me. I was only trying to give a friendly little nibble. Me and her are through.

21st November

May have been a little hasty in my denouncement of Mummy and her boobs yesterday. It turns out that when you refuse any type of milk other than breast milk, then refuse breast milk, you're left with not that much, plus I missed my cosy cuddles with her... so I generously relented in the middle of the night. Mummy seemed really pleased to be woken twice in the night, like the good old days. She's so lucky to have me.

25th November

We were away in the Lakes and had a mixed bag of a weekend.

Positive: I got to hang out with Edie. **Negative:** Lily was there, so I only got any attention from Edie when Lily was sleeping.

Positive: I got told I had the softest cheeks ever by Lily's older sister, Sophie. **Negative:** it meant she was endlessly stroking them.

Positive: I wasn't feeling that great, so didn't have to eat any of Mummy's food that she cooked for the other babies (this is becoming a habit). **Negative:** Mummy force-fed me a yoghurt, as she was scared I wouldn't sleep if I was hungry.

Positives: Force-feeding me a yoghurt led to me explosively vomiting all over the carpet of the house we were staying in, and Mummy and Daddy had to scrub it up and apologise profusely. **Negative:** There is no negative when Mummy and Daddy have to clean up your vom.

Upon reflection, a reasonable trip.

28th November

It turns out that the vomit wasn't induced by yoghurt, but actually I was ill. And I have been for four days. It feels like eternity!

It does mean I got to make Mummy miss only her second Monday back at work, which she said was just "typical", but secretly I could tell she was glad of all the cuddles. And so was I, as when all is said and done, she's pretty good at them, and I like the way she strokes my hair. And then I got to make Daddy miss a day of work. And then I got to spend a day with Grandma and Grandad. And it meant I missed all three days of nursery. A Brucey Bonus, indeed.

I've averaged about eight episodes of *In the Night Garden* daily, interspersed occasionally with *Teletubbies,* to mix things up a bit. And whilst I do love it, there are definitely some disconcerting episodes. Pretty sure Iggle Piggle shouldn't be sneaking into Upsy Daisy's bed (the #metoo campaign mustn't have reached the Night Garden yet). I'm definitely sure that Iggle Piggle should be able to sneeze, and hear a sneeze, without falling down with shock each time. He's obviously of a nervous disposition. And it cannot be healthy for Makka Pakka to live in a cave and just act as a gooseberry between Iggle Piggle and Upsy Daisy all the time. I question the impact this has on all of their mental health.

Anyway, in spite of these concerns, I still fecking love it.

1st December

Holy shit. My life has changed forever. For the better. One word: chocolate.

Mummy didn't seem overly keen about my new discovery, but my ever wilful grandma soon sorted her out and wore her down with "just a little piece won't hurt". You're right, Grandma, it didn't hurt. It was beyond delightful. In fact, I might not eat anything else, ever again. Apparently, I get one every day. Cha-ching!

This momentous occasion took place at something called a "baby shower". Although there was no baby, and I didn't see anyone getting wet. There was just a load of gaggling women, a load of boring presents, and my fatter-by-the-day Auntie Justine with a sparkly sash on. All a bit pointless, if you ask me.

My second-favourite moment, after the chocolate, was when Mummy looked more than a little embarrassed when she had to tell Auntie Justine's seventy-six-year-old nan why she had nicknamed the baby Juan, in front of all the guests. Apparently, it goes really well with their surname: King. I don't get it.

5th December

I'm still going to nursery, and to be honest, I quite like it. I get far better food than Mummy cooks, I get to do crafts which Mummy could never really be arsed to do (apart from the one time she tried to make moon sand and I just ate it), and when I get home, Mummy and Daddy are so tired I get to do whatever the feck I want.

I always like to push it, just to see how far Shannon will go to keep me happy, and today was my best yet; I managed to get her to feed me leek and potato soup using a Calpol syringe. Ha! I thought she'd stop after three different plastic spoons, but no, she persevered with a variety of utensils, until I took it from the syringe.

I heard Mummy whisper, 'Are you fecking kidding me?' as we walked out, so presumably I won't get this treatment at home.

8th December

Had a Christmas party today. Not that I have any clue what Christmas is. I think it's where you get to wear a sparkly dress, Mummy drinks some prosecco, Daddy worries about my naps and sleep, and I get to eat whatever I want as long as I don't kick off too much in front of other people. I think I like Christmas.

9th December

James my betrothed better watch out. I've met an older man. Fraser.

He's three, he's cute, he loves tractors, he can say my name, he doesn't even wear nappies, and he can use a knife and fork. What more could you want?

Well, apart from the fact he lives in the Cayman Islands, and didn't really pay me that much attention, apart from a token offering of a toy at one point, but we'll ignore that for now.

He is my Mummy's friend's little boy, and he's so cool. Probably the coolest person I've ever met. And his Mummy is pretty cool, too. Not sure quite why she's friends with my mummy, but maybe she feels sorry for her.

Anyway, the only downside was that Fraser has a baby sister, and Mummy just wanted to hold her all the time. I mean, I don't want her to hold me, but that doesn't mean she can hold anyone else. I soon put an end to that, and clung to her like a limpet.

Good job there's no new babies on the horizon in our family, as I would not cope.

Month 12:

A Child Is born

12th December

Obviously, the highlight of Mummy's month today, the photoshoot. She caught me off-guard, as normally we do it in the evening, so I have all day to plot my avoidance tactics, but as soon as I was awake and trudged downstairs, *FLASH*, and it was done.

The sneaky bugger must have pre-written it, as I had no prep time whatsoever; not even the tell-tale sign of the felt tip being collected from the drawer.

Next month, I'll be onto it.

15th December

Not sure what was wrong with Mummy today, but she looked and smelled terrible. Her face was all grey/green and she kept moaning about a headache. I actually felt quite sorry for her, as she didn't get in till very late and kept falling over, so she must have some bruises today.

Needless to say, I was the dutiful daughter, and made sure she didn't need to spend a second apart from me all day. At all. I wouldn't let Daddy change my nappy, give me food, hand me water. Anything. I just wanted Mummy.

Oddly, she kept encouraging me to watch TV and lie down, when normally she bangs on about screen time, but I've been listening to her, and I agree that I do need to play more so I duly obliged today and demanded Mummy do the same.

16th December

Mummy seemed marginally brighter today, albeit still a reluctant participant in life, and not overly keen on our shopping trip. Kept moaning something about "this never used to happen when I was nineteen". Not quite sure what this meant but presume it's linked to the greenness of yesterday.

We went with Daddy and Nanny and Uncle Rhys, who has really upped his game recently. He's developed the excellent ability to obey my orders, and has become a top-notch slave. Gone are the days when he would hold me like I was carrying Ebola, and he's more than happy to throw me in the air (sometimes it's a little bit too high and a little bit of wee comes out), and fetch things off the floor when I throw them there on purpose. Ledge.

Anyway, after I had managed to seriously impact the success rate of any actual shopping by whining constantly when in the buggy, and trying to pull items off the shelves when in the carrier, everyone relented, and they each had thirty minutes to complete their shopping whilst they took in it turns to look after me.

We then went for a very posh lunch in a place belonging to a man called Jamie. Something about the shine of the glassware told me that this was the place to really practise my food-launching skills, as well as try to commandeer as much cutlery as possible.

Apparently, it was not the place to do this, but I screamed if anyone tried to stop me, so we left before dessert. Great day all round.

18th December

Hear ye, hear ye, a baby is born. I think Mummy would actually climb onto the rooftops and shout this if she could. It's embarrassing how giddy she is.

Apparently, I have a new baby cousin. I don't know what one is, but it sounds pretty shite.

Although the way Mummy keeps banging on about it and showing me photos of a blanket with a fleshy ball sticking out of it, you'd think it was the second coming. Which I suppose is quite apt, given the time of year.

Anyway, I slapped her in the face with a spoon full of yoghurt, to knock some sense into her, and to remind her she has her own cute bundle of joy right here.

19th December

Had a terrifying experience at nursery today. I had to sit on the knee of a strange man with a red suit and a white beard, whilst everyone smiled about it! Have they not heard of stranger danger?

Needless to say, I gave the appropriate reaction, and screamed in his face, which made people laugh. I don't understand.

I did get given a present, so I suppose there was a silver lining, although Mummy wouldn't let me rip it open and instead made me put it under the huge tree which has suddenly appeared in our lounge. Very frustrating.

22nd December

Today was a rather special day, as I got to see my beloved James after a very long time apart. I couldn't even remember his face, it had been that long. I felt bad about my minor dalliance with the idea of Fraser, but he's long gone, and James is really funny and cute. Unfortunately, his daddy came with him, and he is still really scary. I pretty much hate all men I don't know, but he is one of those 'triers', who wanted me to like him, which made him more annoying, as well as terrifying. He kept trying to tickle me and give me toys.

I just wanted him to sod off.

Anyway, eventually, after I'd screamed in his face and cowered into my own lovely daddy for a while, he left me alone and I was able to focus on reminding James how cool and mature I am.

I started with putting the rings on my pole and made sure to clap myself after each one, and then moved onto standing-not-holding-onto-anything. I even whacked out the old "hold a fake phone to your ear and say ga ga", but he didn't seem bothered. But then I brought out my LED spiky epilepsy-inducing ball (which might actually have been made for dogs) and hooked him in. We battled over it as all young lovebirds do, ending in me gouging his cheek when he stole it from me. I like him, but not that much.

We had a romantic meal for two with both our mummies feeding us, and then he left. He didn't respond at all to my furious waving. He must be playing hard to get.

24th December

Mummy has been banging on about this thing called "Amelia Rose" and "your new baby cousin" for a few days now. They are always said together, so I think they might be the same thing. Anyway, today I got to meet it and, I'll be honest, what a waste of my sodding time. Turns out, it is just a really boring, very small person, that doesn't do anything except make little squeaks every so often. Grandma keeps saying how we are going to best friends, but I can't see it myself. She needs to seriously up her game before I consider it. Although Mummy is besotted, and keeps cuddling me extra hard after she has held her, and saying things like, 'Oh I miss you being like that.' I'm insulted – I was never so ill-equipped for life.

Anyway, I gave a cursory, indifferent stare and then crawled off to play with my Uncle Matt, who is looking quite haggard, I must say. In fact, he looks absolutely, bloody terrible, and wasn't quite as willing to crawl around the house after me as usual. I hope this "Amelia Rose" has nothing to do with it.

Afterwards, we went to a really cold hall, where Mummy's friends were with their vast array of children. I was dressed in a ridiculous Christmas tree tutu outfit, and was feeling pretty stupid until Edie walked in dressed in a full-on Father Christmas costume. I suddenly felt much better.

This was only momentarily, though, as from nowhere, an eight-foot festive woodland creature, the Christmas Squirrel, stormed into the room with bag full of presents. What the frig is a Christmas Squirrel? It was strange, as one of the daddies had gone missing just before the squirrel arrived, and I heard him whisper, 'I can't believe they didn't have a Father Christmas costume.'

I didn't like the hall, it smelt funny. And I didn't like my outfit. And I certainly didn't like the Christmas Squirrel; so I decided to sod it and kick off. I made sure I cried for a good ten minutes, until Daddy conceded and drove me home. I think he was looking for an excuse to leave anyway. He doesn't enjoy small talk.

We left Mummy there, determined to cling on to some festive spirit. I think she was quite upset we missed the annual Christmas photo, though. Apparently, she's been waiting years to have a baby to hold on it.

We finished the day with Nanny and Uncle Rhys, and everyone got very excited when I got changed into my pyjamas and got given a box with a teddy and a book in it. Mummy kept harping on about "the starting of traditions" and looked all glassy-eyed. She's such a melt.

25th December

What a day I have had. It's been amazing! I have seen all my favourite people, and eaten five chocolate buttons, and a chocolate from Grandma's tree, and got to play with lots of new toys. Possibly most exciting of all, I met Makka Pakka and Iggle Piggle. I thought they'd be bigger in real life, and I didn't think you'd have to press their tummies to make them sing, but they were still great.

Because I'd had such a lovely day, I really didn't want to go to bed. So I did loads of whingeing and managed to get back up and play with everybody, not just once but twice. I decided to show off to Amelia Rose, and remind everybody else how clever I am, so was diving all over her little bed and trying to jump on Uncle Matt, and kissing all my teddies, and generally racing around. It was just the best.

27th December

After a mystery disappearance, my ride-on princess car is back, and it is epic. I can use it to help me walk. I can use it to be pushed about on. I can use it to wind everybody up, as the music is so annoying. Immense.

It's helped me cheer up a bit, as I was feeling mega tired and gloomy after a rough night.

I woke about 00:30, when I heard Mummy come to bed, and then just couldn't get comfortable whenever I lay down. I can't put my finger on it but it just hurt a bit.

However, if I sat up... awesome, no pain at all. So that's what I did. For just over three hours. Here's how it went:

00:30 Wake up, sit up, chatter loudly to myself.

00:45 Daddy comes in and tries to settle me. Lie down. Hurts. Sit up again. Repeat for twenty minutes.

01:05 Mummy comes in and whacks out the boob. Delicious but, if anything, the glug of energy woke me up further.

01:20 After I hit Mummy in the face, she put me back into bed and wrongly assumes singing *Twinkle, Twinkle Little Star* will signal it's time for me to sleep. Still can't lie down, as it hurts. Sit and chatter for ten minutes.

01:30 Bored of chattering, decide to shout.

01:33 Daddy silently enters the room, picks me up, and takes me to their room.

01:55 After twenty-two minutes of lying in the dark, trying to lull me to sleep whilst I hit alternate parents in the face, breasts or testicles, they whisper, 'This isn't working, she's being a tit, put her back in her own bed.' Upon which, I continually cycle between sitting up and chattering, and lying down and moaning in discomfort

02:30 Mummy re-enters the room and whacks out the other boob. Have a little bit, but it tastes of mild desperation.

02:35 Mummy brings me back into their bed. I go back to alternate body-part slapping.

02:40 Daddy says, 'Sod it!' and puts *In the Night Garden* on his phone.

02:44 Daddy falls asleep, so Mummy has to play it on her phone.

02:48 Every four minutes, Mummy has to awake from her light doze, and skip ads, as she forgot she could play it on iPlayer and uses YouTube instead. Continue for two episodes.

03:27 Mummy places me back into bed.

03:33 After six minutes of moaning as I try to sleep in spite of the increasing pain, Mummy enters with Calpol.

03:43 Calpol begins to kick in and I drop off to sleep.

A valuable lesson has been learnt all round: if in doubt, Calpol.

30th December

Another day, another random excuse for a party – today it was "Christmas family games".

From what I can gather, every living, UK-based member of my maternal family – even a cousin of Grandma's – come to Grandma's, get given a coloured sticker, and compete in an endless number of pointless games. I even got a sticker, which was pretty redundant, as I can't play carpet boules, air hockey, the memory game, or Who Wants to be a Millionaire? So I ate it. Or at least tried to, before Daddy caught me and fished it out.

I've not been feeling that great over the last couple of days, and I have such a pain in my ears, so I was suitably, and understandably, grumpy, with everyone at the party, independent of what team they were on.

In the spirit of charades, I kept trying to show them how crap I felt, but they're fecking useless. I'm tugging at my ear constantly, but they just keep saying, 'Yes, that's right, that's your head, clever girl!'

Yes, I know it's my fecking head, you fecking morons, and yes, I am clever, unlike you, who can't even understand your daughter's ear is about to fall off. Probably.

Really struggled to get to sleep and Mummy and Daddy were swearing and stomping about and shoving nipples in my mouth (mainly Mummy, but I reckon Daddy would try if he thought it would work) and complaining. God, they're frustrating!!!

31st December

Woke up with all my hair and ear covered in gunk. My ear drum has perforated. Shocker! And man, it feels better.

What feels even better is my sense of righteousness. Mummy is kicking herself about the fact they've been moaning about me and my grumpiness, when actually it was for a very valid reason. So I have got to do whatever I want today. Which is excellent, as I feel absolutely on top of the world now, so can take full advantage. Even managed to gouge a fair chunk out of Mummy's mouth before, and she didn't shout at me.

And what tastes even better is the antibiotics. Banana flavour? Bright yellow to ensure maximum staining of most clothing? Slightly grainy texture? What's not to love?

I am ending the year on a high.

2nd January

Went to nursery today. Which was fine.

What is not fine is the fact Mummy didn't have work. So much for all those tears about missing out on precious moments together back in November. Soon forgot their salty taste, didn't she?

I mean, I had a great time, and even Lucas didn't piss me off that much, but still. It's the principle.

3rd January

My friend Sylvia from NCT is a bloody legend. Definitely something to aspire to. An idol, if you will.

Firstly, she's a real free spirit. Independent. Happy to wander off into soft play all by herself. I like that in a friend.

Secondly, she's almost walking, which makes Mummy feel like I should be walking, as Sylvia is younger than me. I always like it when Mummy has that bit of parenting self-doubt.

Thirdly, and most importantly, she just doesn't give a shite about anything.

Today, she just crawled/teetered/wobbled over to some random person's table, crawled under the seat, and licked the bottom of all their shoes. If that's not living your best life, I really don't know what is.

5th January

Another day, another soft play. I feel this is Mummy's sole idea of how to entertain me these days. I mean, I'm not complaining, as I love it. Balls to lick, slides to slide down, food crumbs to hoover up, all whilst requiring constant Mummy supervision, are a winner for me.

We went for Jasper "the trendy one's" birthday, and had a fabulous time. James wasn't there to continue our romance, but Sophie and Sylvia the shoe-licker were all there, and I have to admit it was nice to have a bit of girl time.

Daddy was, obviously (Mummy kept saying this whenever she explained where Daddy was), playing golf again, *again*, so it was just the two of us, with the other NCT crew. And actually, it was really nice. She's not a bad egg, really, and she's definitely in the top three of NCT mums' league table for playing fun games. James' mummy is top.

In addition to her a-bit-better-than-mediocre-at-playing, Mummy is also so awkward, it's hilarious. She kept noticing people she went to school with, and trying to avoid them at all costs. Including diving into the ball pool, and hiding in a tunnel. They probably won't remember her anyway, as she's pretty bland, so I don't know why she bothers. All because she knows she'll go bright red and stammer when she sees them. She needs to chill out and be more Sylvia.

10th January

Had a mega busy few days at nursery, and Lucas has gone back to pissing me off, as he keeps pushing me over and poking me when Shannon isn't looking, so I was so excited to see Grandma and Grandad today. Although they obviously got the same memo as Mummy, about the joys of soft play, so off we went to another one. You'd think I'd tire of them, but no, I just love climbing up to the slide. And sliding down the slide. And climbing up to the slide. And sliding down the slide. And climbing up to the slide. And sliding down the slide. You get the picture. I think Grandad really loved the repetitiveness of it, too.

Grandad also had to contend with some toddler twins that latched onto him, and kept wanting him to help them get up the slide. Now, my Grandad is a lovely, very non-confrontational, tolerant man, but even I could tell he was going to lose his shit as the twins' daddy was just sat playing Angry Birds on his phone, whilst Grandad had three children, two of which he had no duty of care for, hanging off him.

In the end, Grandad took me to the sensory room, slammed the door, and pretended we weren't in there, whilst the twins tried to sabotage the code-encrypted door. Luckily, they had a similar attention span to a pair of gnats with ADHD, so our escape was successful.

As they dropped me back off with Mummy, Grandma

and Grandad said, 'See you on the big day!' I literally have no idea what they are talking about. Maybe my betrothal to James is finally coming to fruition and we're getting married. Mummy does keep mentioning a lovely new dress for my special day.

From M&S.

Obviously.

One

Well, they've only gone and bloody done it! In spite of some serious concerns at the start of all of this, my parents have kept me alive for a whole year. Admittedly, there have been a few mishaps, but fair play to them. I'm alive. With two fully functioning nostrils, an "inny" belly button, a nose that has returned to its normal cuteness, and no long-term damage from being hit on the head by a fridge door as a new-born. Result.

We celebrated with a birthday party, which was quite the social event. Obviously, Mummy invested too much time into printing photos of my monthly updates, and carefully sticking them onto a decorative timeline, which no one actually took any notice of. And obviously she invited all my family and "friends" (basically her and Daddy's friends with kids), so it was crowded and hot, and so fecking loud. And obviously she drank that second glass of prosecco that took her into being a bit tipsy. But it was actually quite fun.

Who knew having all your favourite people in one place could be so nice?

There was a suspicious streak of brown left on my new slide, which we are all hoping was the chocolate cake, and at one point, at least three children were eating Doritos straight from the floor under the table, but all in all, it was a success.

After everyone had gone, and I was modelling my new nursery backpack, whilst riding my princess carriage of destruction and looking oh-so-grown-up, I looked over and Mummy was rubbing her tummy, looking quite emotional.

Daddy looked quite emotional too as he said, 'Maybe it won't be so hard next time.'

Author's notes

I'm not really sure what to write here, but it seemed a little weird having written the book as Emily, but then not to have said a bit about myself. I know I would have wanted to find out my take on things if I was reading this book (if that makes any sense), so here is my bit. And maybe, hopefully, it might help some people feel a bit better about what they feel/felt when in possession of a new baby⋯ So here goes⋯ a bit from me⋯

I wanted to be a mum so much. Since I was little. And I felt so lucky to get pregnant, and despite feeling quite sick in the first trimester, really quite enjoyed the experience. Apart from the piles towards the end, that is. Horrific. Cried a few times about them.

Anyway, I was also lucky with my birth, overall. I mean, it was fecking horrendous and painful, but I laboured "well" (thank the lord for diamorphine) and needed some stitches, which I had prepared myself for, as I had made all my friends tell me about their births in full gory detail. I even made a deal with myself that I'd take a second-degree tear from the outset (I felt no tear would be asking too much, but I did not want a third-degree!) and was quite happy when the midwife confirmed it was one. What I was not prepared for was the feeling of complete helplessness and "what the feck" ness I experienced.

When they first placed Emily on top of me, she was gross. She was covered in my blood, and vernix, and god-knows-what-else, and really was a bit minging, if I'm honest (maybe after a waterbirth they look a bit better – I'll ask Philippa!). This feeling just kind of continued, and I would just stare at her for ages, at a loss as to what I felt, and what to do, apart from shoving a nipple up her nose every so often, in the hope it would end up in her mouth; analysing her latch (which I knew nothing about); checking for a blue line on her nappy religiously, and then staring at her some more.

My milk came in around day two/three, and then I bled on the bathmat after a bath to try and soothe my stitches and even more painful piles (apologies, I'm an over-sharer), and I remember bringing it down to put in the washing machine (it was white, there was no hope, and completely my fault, because who has a white bathmat?!) and I just burst into tears because I felt so completely numb. I had wanted her for so long, and now she was here I was clueless and helpless, and it felt shite.

I finally plucked up the courage to message a few close friends and tentatively led up to saying, 'I don't think I love my baby,' and I'm so glad I did. Most of them messaged back and said they had felt the same. One of my close friends said, 'The first two weeks are all about survival,' and it was possibly the best thing I had ever heard, so that's what I did. And we survived, and it got better. (Come to think of it, the same friend gave me wedding advice of 'Try and do one thing each day that makes the other person's life that little bit easier,' and that's pretty epic, too. Maybe she should write a book.)

I was shocked by my emotions, or lack of them; particularly when everyone else seemed to feel so happy, and I was worried that this was some sort of post-natal depression, but it wasn't, and although that can be a sign (I am by no means a mental health expert), it seems to me that it is also quite normal to feel like that, without it being a serious issue. So now when people I know near their time to give birth, I always say, 'Don't worry if you don't love them straight away,' which seems an odd thing to say to someone who is so excited about the imminent arrival of their bundle of joy, and I tend to get some weird looks, but it's something I wish someone had said to me. And people have said thanks afterwards.

(Although I did it to someone once when I was pissed at the races and I didn't really know her, and it didn't go down very well at all. So maybe I should know my audience a bit better.)

So yes, once I realised I did love her, I stopped worrying about it (I am a massive over-thinker as well as an over-sharer), and that bit became easier. What didn't become easier for ages was the bloody anxiety about her dying. All the time. Feck me, why did they make babies' breathing so bloody unpredictable, even when they're fit and well? I am a science teacher, my parents are doctors, I know it's highly unlikely that a baby will literally just stop breathing. But bugger me, it's like they're made to test you. I remember at about three weeks old, the day before Emily went into hospital for the first time in the ambulance, I was so worried about this cold she had, and I suddenly thought, 'Shit, she's going to learn to drive one day.' How parents cope with that, I have no idea. Emily is just going to ride a bike. And never go on nights out. Or to Malia in a mixed group of thirty when she's eighteen. As an aside, I knew something was wrong with her then, and I couldn't stop crying, because I couldn't put my finger on it, and everyone said I was being silly. Well, they soon shut up when we were in hospital, and I was so relieved that I went with my gut and called 111. I didn't even know I had a gut instinct and when people said, 'You know your baby best,' I did not believe them, but it turned out to be true, so always trust yourself.

So yes, the anxiety and worry is pretty terrifying, but it does become more manageable as they become more robust. When we were in the hospital when she was six weeks old, even just three weeks after that first time, it felt less daunting, because she seemed that bit stronger.

What else…? Oh, the boredom. Wow! I struggled with that. Before having a baby, I thought I loved being around babies. But it turns out I love being around babies for about two hours, when I can then give them back. Having one ALL of the time is really hard, and I found it boring.

And then felt guilty for finding it boring. Particularly when they are about four to five months old, so can't really do anything, but still need entertaining. When we'd have a rare morning at home, I'd have to set challenges for myself and see if I could not look at the time for a whole ten minutes. I rarely managed it, and I'd really try. I'd have done two stories, some tummy time, some dangling objects to be hit, some nursery rhymes, and still only eight bloody minutes had passed!

Luckily, my closest NCT friend admitted she found it boring, and then I felt much better. In the book, you'll notice we never spent a day in the house. Maybe just one, when she was ill. I could not cope with it. I dislike my own company, and need to be around people, so made sure I did at least one thing that got me out of the house every day. Often, I would overbook, and be rushing around, which then made life more difficult but heyho, you live and learn. Not everyone is the same, but I think the power of a cup of tea and meet-up with someone is so undervalued. Although maybe we do appreciate it more, in the aftermath of lockdowns, when we have experienced not being allowed to do it.

I don't want to give you my life story (I've shared way too much already), but the final thing that I will mention is breastfeeding. I breastfed Emily because all my friends had breastfed their babies, so it was the "norm". All the midwives told me I had to, and I am inherently a rule-follower, so I did. I am also incredibly stubborn, which is why I stuck with it. The first few weeks were agony, but Emily was gaining weight like a trooper. However, I knew something wasn't right. I suggested tongue tie to a few people, but got rebuffed, so stuck at it, but in the end I pushed for someone to come to the house from a breastfeeding charity group in our area, and they diagnosed it.

I felt so bloody validated as up until this point, I just felt so clueless and, because she was gaining weight, it felt like people were ignoring me. We got it snipped, which I promise is way worse for you than them, and things got better. I soon stopped caring about people seeing a stray nipple, and breastfeeding in public was fine for me (I did once leave my nipple hanging out through a breastfeeding top-slit in the middle of a pub for about five minutes, so after that, I really didn' t give one).

The thing that then got me was everyone seemed to need to explain their feeding choice at baby groups, etc. The number of times I heard, "I fed him for the first eight weeks, but then we had to go to a bottle…" and, "I tried so hard but it just wouldn't work" made me sad. Sad that people felt they needed to justify their choices and decisions, which were often out of their hands. One of my NCT friends couldn't breastfeed and she felt so sad and guilty about it. It was awful. What's worse is that if I met up with another breastfeeding mum but Emily hadn't fed in that time, I would find a way to drop it into conversation (I wouldn't if the other baby was bottle-fed). I still don't know why I felt the need to do that, and I'm angry at myself for it, as really it's showing off about something that shouldn't be showed off about. Maybe because I was proud of myself. But by doing that, I was still making it a thing. And it isn't. What I'm trying to say is, however you feed your baby, it's fine. You're feeding them, which is amazing, and many organisms in the animal kingdom don't even bother with that.

As I mentioned earlier, talking to people helped me a lot. There are so many Instagram pages and books and Facebook groups now for new mums, which I think is amazing overall and I did find some of these reassuring. But some of them really pissed me off. The really bloody crafty ones are the worst. And the ones who love tummy fecking time. And many were not telling the truth, which I suppose is why I started Emily's hand-written "alternative milestones" cards, that eventually led to the book, as people liked them so much. I think the truth is actually funnier.

Anyway, I found I talked a lot to my existing friends who had babies, my wonderful mum (with caution, she was brilliant in so many ways and I couldn't have coped without her, but she also had some very strong opinions on certain things, i.e. dummies!), and my NCT group, who were an invaluable source of support. I feel very lucky to have paid for such lovely middle-class friends and for them to have turned out to be pretty epic (Phillipa is actually fictitious; we were lucky as a group not to have anyone like her, but I did come across mums like that, who just made you feel inept) . I remember the moment when one of them said, 'What's the worst thing you've called your baby? Mine is twat!' and the sense of relief, and the feeling that I had found my people, was immense, and much-needed. So I would definitely recommend talking to other mums, and being honest, as you'll hopefully be pleasantly surprised by what you hear back!

I've rambled on for ages now, so I'll leave it here. I truly hope you enjoyed the book, and that some of it rings true for you, and it maybe even made you smile.

Babies are little feckers. But they're cute (apart from just after birth, when they're gross), and amazing, and frustrating, and truly wonderful, all at the same time.

My friend sent me a quote in the early days that said something like "the days are long, but the years are short", and this is so true. Sometimes, even the seconds seem long, and it is so bloody hard.

And the mum-guilt is unlike anything else you'll ever know. And it is so overwhelmingly relentless. But as long as you're doing your best, you're doing an awesome job. And that little hand on yours, or neck-nuzzle, or laugh, is so, so worth it.

Thank yous

Not wanting to turn this into an Oscars winner's speech, I would like to thank a few people.

Firstly, my awesome friends. I'm not going to name you all, as I'm then at risk of missing someone out, and that would be awful, but you know who you are. 2020 was a pretty tough one but you will never know how much you helped me get through it. And now we can have playdates in each other's houses again, rather than freezing our tits off in gardens and parks, and it is just wonderful. Yay!

Secondly, my publisher, Katharine. Your help and guidance throughout this process has been amazing and this book would not exist without you.

Finally, my family. You're pretty epic, really! Your unwavering support and utter belief in me are incredible and so appreciated.

So thank you all.

Printed in Great Britain
by Amazon

79175170R00159